MW01129180

The Mexican Revolution

A Captivating Guide to the Mexican Civil War and How Pancho Villa and Emiliano Zapata Impacted Mexico

Free Bonus from Captivating History
(Available for a Limited time)

Hi History Lovers!

Now you have a chance to join our exclusive history list so you can get your first history ebook for free as well as discounts and a potential to get more history books for free! Simply visit the link below to join.

<u>Captivatinghistory.com/ebook</u>

Also, make sure to follow us on Facebook, Twitter and Youtube by searching for Captivating History.

Contents

Introduction

The Mexican Revolution was a defining moment of the 20th century. The Mexican fight for democracy, equality, and justice sent shockwaves around the world. No other episode in its history has left a deeper mark. It is a three-act drama full of politics, persecution, and war, not to mention earthquakes, signs in the sky, and even spiritualist sessions, while being populated by larger-than-life villains, international spies, and the universally known figures of Pancho Villa and Emiliano Zapata. In fact, our modern idea of "revolution" owes much to what happened in this country between 1910 and 1920.

Although the uprisings of the oppressed classes have occurred since antiquity, Mexico in the 20th century is a unique case—this was the first triumphant popular revolution that, unlike others, was able to establish a popular government that carried out extensive social transformations without resorting to state terror, as was the case in the Soviet Union and China. It integrated marginalized groups into national life, and it gave birth to a refurbished nation, where, for a hundred years, there has not been a new coup d'état, a problem that devastated other Latin American countries during the 20th century. In a way, the course of the First World War was defined through Mexico, and the ideological expressions that emerged during that decade, such as the Plan of Ayala and the 1917 Constitution, influenced movements as far away as the Russian Revolution, the Republic of Weimar, and the Zapatista uprising of 1994. Several Central American insurrections in the last quarter of the 20th century owe much to its influence.

Hence, the Mexican Revolution has been an inexhaustible well for historians and novelists. Books in various languages could fill a large library, from the first accounts when the roar of the cannons had barely died down to the third decade of the 21st century, which has already seen the appearance of new volumes and biographies. The books entitled "A Short History..." of the Mexican Revolution, or something of the like, are legion. One of the most interesting aspects of the Mexican Revolution is that it was one of the first wars in the world to be widely documented through photography and cinema. Emiliano Zapata, in the imagination of the inhabitants of Mexico City, was the "Mexican Attila," a savage from the mountains leading hordes of bandits who raped and destroyed, which is something that the press of the capital deliberately fabricated. When Zapata's peasant army finally marched into the city, the citizens found that the reality was quite different.

Finally, the Mexican Revolution was not just one more war in a long list but an almost genetic transformation of the nation that, in its aftermath, was able to create a cultural and intellectual movement that formed the identity of what is now recognized as typically "Mexican," such as Diego Rivera's murals and Saturnino Herrán's paintings, the music of Manuel M. Ponce, and the novels of Mariano Azuela.

This book by *Captivating History* appears in the year of the hundredth anniversary of the end of the Mexican Revolution and is a handy guide for the neophyte reader who wants to learn everything from scratch.

Chapter 1 – The Comet

"By the time the comet appears on the western horizon, after May 20, it will present a spectacle so magnificent and astonishing that we must remember it as one of the great events of our lives, and in later years we will speak to our grandchildren of the great year of 1910."

El Faro, April 15, 1910, a few months before the Mexican Revolution began

A small comet popped up in the sky of Mexico City in the early hours before dawn. It flew across the winter firmament, which at that time was particularly bright and clear. It was hardly a blotch in the sky. At first, only the astronomers—a profession that Mexico had had since the time of the Mayas—showed interest in the return of Halley's Comet. But 1910 was going to be a spectacular sighting. By the beginning of May, the star and its tail crossed the vault of heaven from horizon to horizon, and it was visible even at midday. Even in our times, the appearance of a comet can cause anxiety in some people. It was no wonder that at the dawn of the 20th century, it was seen as an ominous sign by most Mexicans, those rural people who worked from sunrise to sunset and who, for the most part, were poor and illiterate. The older men and women said that it was a sign that a calamity was coming, just as in ancient times when a comet had announced the fall of Montezuma's empire before the arrival of the Spaniards.

In the spring of 1910, panic spread, not only among the poor and illiterate, when the scientific community announced that in mid-May, Earth would pass through the gaseous tail of the comet. It is unclear where the pernicious rumor started, which was widely reproduced in the newspapers of the time, that Halley's *cauda* (Latin for "tail") contained poisonous cyanogen gas that would exterminate all humanity. The news spread like a pandemic, although the most serious scientists reported that this would not be the case—some said that the tail would only give people the effect of laughing gas and that, in the worst-case scenario, humanity would just be laughing their brains out during the encounter.

But it was too late. By then, those who knew how natural phenomena worked said that the comet would collide with Earth, that the tail was toxic, or that gravitational forces would create destructive tides in every continent. Those who did not know about physics simply had a feeling that the wandering star was an omen and that a major affliction was going to fall on Mexico. Maybe a great war. Or the plague. On the day set for the encounter between the planet and the comet, on May 18th, to be precise, the churches across Mexico were crowded with people seeking confession, believing that the end was near. But as the parishioners lined up in front of the confessionals, surely no one knew that the danger had, in fact, already passed. At nine o'clock in the morning, without anyone noticing, the world passed through the tail of the most famous comet in history. On May 19th, the newspapers reported with relief that the predictions had failed. But the older men and women knew better.

Ten years after the comet, in 1920, the date when most historians place the end of the Mexican Revolution, 10 to 20 percent of the Mexicans had died, and little was left of that 19th-century country, which had seen Halley's Comet with astonished eyes. Its fields, haciendas, and villages were semi-destroyed, the bulletproof adobe walls of the houses punctured with holes, and people trembled at the sight of a group of men on horseback. Bridges, roads, and telegraph poles were shattered in many places. Even worse, almost every single family had at least one member missing due to some battle, the hundreds of executions that took place, thousands of self-exiles, women being seized by parties of horsemen, or deaths from disease and hunger. Between two to three million people, including both military and civilian statistics, had died, and blood soaked the fields in the north, center, and south of the country. This is a shocking figure if one considers that this number represented around 20 percent of the population at that time. Several presidents had passed through the National Palace in Mexico City, including one whose tenure only lasted 45 minutes, and the newspapers had reported two assassinations. It was not the tail of a comet that swept Mexico but rather a wind saturated with the voices of indignation, rage, criticism, and, above all, the demand for justice.

A revolution that had timidly begun as a democratic movement became a major economic and social upheaval that changed the face of the country. Ten years after Halley's Comet, a traveler would have seen a different Mexico. For a decade, the world watched the Mexican Revolution closely, the first important war to be extensively photographed, filmed, and reported on. In that time, from 1910 to 1920, Mexico had also gone through two invasions by the United States and became involved in a diplomatic affair with Germany that launched America into the First World War.

The storm that swept Mexico also ousted the old oligarchy and its army, built the foundations of government to end the servitude of the workers, and created the opportunity to redefine Mexico as a more egalitarian society. Even though it was half destroyed and still smelling of gunpowder, travelers who visited the country in 1920 would have noticed extensive devastation and a people fed up with the war but also something impalpable: the Mexican Revolution, with its two million deaths, had marked the route that would guide Mexico through the rest of the 20th century toward an ample agrarian reform, a popular and nationalist state, and, after a hundred years, a country that could, at last, aspire to live in peace.

But what had caused such a storm when no one could imagine in 1910 that a popular uprising—let alone a nationwide full-blown revolution—could take place in Mexico?

* * *

The year 1910 was marked by celebrations. The government spared no expense to celebrate the hundredth anniversary of the Mexican War of Independence of 1810. In control of the presidency was Porfirio Díaz, an old soldier who had fought against the French in the famous battle of Cinco de Mayo in Puebla, and he had ruled the country with a heavy hand for more than thirty years. For the centennial celebrations, he invited foreign representatives from every corner of the world to see a revamped Mexico City, complete with new monuments reminiscent of national glories, palaces, public facilities, and the jewel of the city—the new mercury streetlights. At the National Palace, there were lavish receptions with Mexican waitresses perfectly chosen to pass as foreigners—namely as blondes. A monument to George Washington was unveiled at one of them, and on September 16th, on Independence Day, the people behind the police lines marveled at a splendid parade with cars and floats that showed the history of Mexico, from Emperor Moctezuma and the great Tenochtitlán to the fight for independence and effigies of past heroes. In Chapultepec Forest, a new lake was inaugurated, and the people witnessed the march of foreign troops saluting Mexico, even France's *Pantalons Rouges*, against whom President Díaz had fought on Cinco de Mayo. The French envoy had a token of admiration and friendship for the old dictator, as he returned the keys of Mexico City, which his predecessor had received from Díaz's enemies in 1863. On September 23rd, which many considered the high point of the celebrations, a lavish dance was held at the National Palace, with 2,000 guests in attendance from all over the world. "I look at Porfirio Diaz, the President of Mexico, as one of the greatest men to be held up for the hero-worship of mankind," said US Secretary of State Elihu Root.

All of this happened in Mexico City, a very small portion of the national territory. But just as a hot air balloon floats up to discover the fields and small towns beyond, the attentive traveler could see, as he moved away from the big city, that Mexico was far from being Díaz's paradise of "Order and Progress," where foreign representatives toasted champagne in cut-glass wineglasses.

Chapter 2 – The Strong Man of the Americas

"Revolution *(noun)* — A major, sudden, and hence typically violent alteration in government and in related associations and structures. / A challenge to the established political order and the eventual establishment of a new order radically different from the preceding one."

—Encyclopedia Britannica

"I don't need lawyers. I need farmhands."

—Luis Terrazas, the richest landowner in Mexico, when they told him they wanted to put schools in his haciendas.

In his youth, Porfirio Díaz had been the hero of Mexico. When France invaded Mexico in 1862, seeking to establish a monarchy, Díaz was a spirited young general who showed heroic behavior in the famous battle of Cinco de Mayo, which is the most popular Mexican holiday in the world, though not in Mexico. After the French were defeated on the outskirts of Puebla, General Díaz chased them with his cavalry to finish them off, despite orders from his commanding general, Ignacio Zaragoza, to leave off. Díaz's comrades were able to make him come back only when Zaragoza threatened to sanction him. Five years later, after the fall of the monarchy of Maximilian of

Habsburg, Díaz had the glory of capturing the capital and marching into Mexico City, an event known as the Reestablishment of the Republic. Later, in 1877, Díaz became the president of the country he had helped save, and except for a brief interim of four years, he ruled Mexico for three decades without interruption under democratic appearances. He organized elections, but he had dismantled the opposition, eliminated his political rivals, put his friends in Congress and state governorships, and won election after election.

Porfirio Díaz is a controversial character in Mexico. Until recently, he was officially the villain of the story, but in recent years, historians have vindicated him to some degree. Díaz was a man of his time. As the president of a country destabilized by a series of coups and incessant local revolts, which threatened to dismember the nation, he managed to finally cut the cycle of coups and local guerrillas, giving Mexico a stability it had never known. During his tenure, known as the Porfiriato, foreign investment flowed into the country, and necessary infrastructure was built, especially railways, roads, and telegraphs. When Díaz took over Mexico, the country had 640 kilometers (almost 400 miles) of railroad tracks. In 1910, at the end of his term, there were almost 20,000 kilometers (close to 12,430 miles) of tracks, which was enough to get from Mexico City to Moscow and back. Before his time, Mexico was a collection of disconnected regions, which, thanks to the railroad, began to feel united and form something more like a nation. Foreign investment, especially American, developed mines and textile industries and exported agriculture, such as coffee, sugar, and henequen. For the first time, there was readily available employment, and real wages increased in one generation. Díaz paid off Mexico's foreign debt, something that had caused Mexico many headaches and foreign interventions in the past, and pacified the troubled areas of the Yucatan Peninsula and the northern border states, which had been devastated throughout the 19th century by the Apache incursions and other ethnic groups. In the international arena, Mexico joined globalization and established good diplomatic relations with powers from around the world. On each one of his birthdays, Díaz received congratulations from the Kaiser, the president of the United States, and the European monarchs. Don Porfirio was the first to meet with a president of the United States, William Taft, in El Paso-Ciudad Juárez. "You are, to my knowledge," said the old general to his chunky neighbor, "the first US premier to visit this land." For all these reasons, Díaz was called the Strong Man of the Americas.

But that prosperity was built upon impoverished and dissatisfied masses. With the turn of the century, the deficiencies of the period, known as Porfirismo, began to emerge like corpses thrown into a lake with the hope that they would not be trouble in the future. Mexico certainly had an incipient industry, but the mining, railroad, large-scale agriculture, and financial sectors were in foreign hands, mainly American. Resentment was rampant both among the middle classes—who received fewer wages than American workers who did the same jobs—and the peasantry. To maintain calm and peace, Díaz had eliminated the freedom of the press, political parties, unions, and anyone who opposed him by any means necessary, including exile and murder. The first death rattles of the regime began in 1906 and 1907. In those years, two strikes broke out in the mining company of Cananea and a textile company named Río Blanco. Despite the fact that the strikers, unwilling to tolerate more injustice and mistreatment by their foreign masters, begged President Díaz to intercede, the general brutally repressed the workers. In the Río Blanco factory, located in the state of Veracruz, gunshots were heard for several days as the forces of order liquidated the strikers, who fled to the hills.

Díaz, of course, was not unaware of the country's situation, the widespread fears that the United States would appropriate more territory, and the dissatisfaction with the attitude of the country's real owners. Mexico's dependence on the business cycle of the United States, as well as Theodore Roosevelt's "big stick" policy, his corollary to the Monroe Doctrine, worried President Díaz so much that in his later years, he began to approach European investors in order to shield Mexico from US annexationist ideology, which had become so strident that it had its hungry eyes on Mexico's northern states. Porfirio Díaz is credited with the phrase that sums up his concern for the neighbor to the north: "Poor Mexico, so far from God and so close to the United States!"

Throughout its history as an independent nation, Mexico had attracted the interests of the great powers due to its geographical position and natural resources. At the beginning of the 20th century, large oil fields were discovered, and Mexico became the world's third-largest producer of what is known as liquid gold. Díaz granted liberal concessions for its exploitation, which made the country even more desirable for foreign investors. Mexico's gold and silver mineral riches were legendary. And the demand for Mexican crops, such as coffee, rubber, and henequen, aroused the greed of international capitalists. As world demand increased and foreign powers expanded their economic interests around the globe, Mexico was on its way to becoming the battlefield of great global interests.

But the most immediate cause for the coming collapse of the old regime was the situation of the rural class, which made up the vast majority of the country. The peasants, chained to large plantations in the south of the country, lived in semi-slavery, suffering physical abuse, and they were indebted for life due to the haciendas, as the bosses paid in kind, never in cash. The peasants' debts were inherited from parents to children, which only perpetuated poverty and despair. American writer John Kenneth Turner, who visited a henequen hacienda in Yucatan during the Porfiriato, was horrified by what he saw.

> Here and there among them I saw tired-looking women and children, sometimes little girls as young as eight or ten. Two thousand [henequen] leaves a day is the usual stint on [the hacienda of] San Antonio Yaxche. On other plantations I was told that it is sometimes as high as three thousand. "We come to work gladly," said another young Maya, "because we're starved. But before the end of the first week we want to run away. That is why they lock us up at night."

The first thing Turner saw on a henequen plantation was how a "slave" was whipped fifty times with a wet rope. "I saw no punishments worse than beating in Yucatan," he wrote. Women were forced to kneel when they were whipped.

The situation of the peasants is key to understanding the Mexican Revolution. By 1910, the year of Halley's Comet, land appropriation and the dispossession of communities at the hands of large landowners and the so-called delimitation companies had been going on for decades. A single family, the Terrazas of Chihuahua, owned seven million hectares alone. There are countries in the world that are smaller than that. Dispossessed peasants came to the planters to offer the only thing they had left: their hands and their work. In the eyes of the country's ruling class, they were a burden, an ignorant and lazy mass that were meant to be oppressed, subjugated, and exploited to death under the sun. "We were tough," admitted Díaz. "The poor are so ignorant that they have no power. We were tough sometimes to the point of being cruel. But all of this was necessary for the life and progress of the nation."

In 1907 and 1908, a sudden American recession that had begun on Wall Street reached Mexico, which, at this point, was highly dependent on the United States' economic cycle. Although the crisis was short-lived in America, the consequences were catastrophic for the Mexicans, who saw prices of consumption goods double while real wages fell to the floor.

The Creelman Interview

In 1908, on the eve of a new presidential election, the nearly eighty-year-old General Díaz gave an interview to a foreign journalist called James Creelman for an American monthly publication called *Pearson's Magazine*. The title of the interview was "Porfirio Díaz: Hero of the Americas," and the journalist did not hide his admiration toward the president. Creelman simply reflected the widespread idea of Díaz among industrialized nations:

There is not a more romantic or heroic figure in all the world, nor one more intensely watched by both the friends and foes of democracy, than the soldier-statesman whose adventurous youth pales the pages of Dumas, and whose iron rule has converted the warring, ignorant, superstitious and impoverished masses of Mexico, oppressed by centuries of Spanish cruelty and greed, into a strong, steady, peaceful, debt-paying and progressive nation.

Creelman forgot to mention that Díaz was a dictator who ferociously repressed any opposition.

But perhaps Creelman didn't mention it because the old general made a startling statement during the historic interview. "I can lay down the Presidency of Mexico without a pang of regret," Díaz said at the outset. Don Porfirio conceded that he had had enough and that he would welcome the emergence of an opposition party. When the interview came out, the text was read with astonished eyes by the Mexican political class. "I will welcome an opposition party. If it appears, I will see it as a blessing and not as an evil, and if it can develop power, not to exploit but to rule, I will stand by it, support it, advise it and forget myself in the successful inauguration of complete democratic government in the country." And it would be through this sudden fissure that Díaz opened that the person of the year of 1911 would make his entry: Francisco Ignacio Madero.

Chapter 3 – Francisco and the Spirits

"My friends, pulque is the best auxiliary of the dictatorship, because it degrades and it brutalizes the peoples and delivers them tied, by their hands and feet, to their executioners."

—Francisco I. Madero

The space of freedom that Díaz opened in the twenty-fourth year of his presidency could have been a moment of lucidity or perhaps a calculated move to defeat his strongest opponent, thus causing a flood of small political parties. The fact is the loophole was exploited by an improbable character, not by a peasant leader in arms, nor by an anarchist worker leader or a communist intellectual. Rather, it was by the son of one of the richest families in the country, Francisco I. Madero.

Francisco Madero was a petite man with an ample forehead, a goatee, and thick eyebrows. He was 1.57 meters tall (around 5'1") and had a deep look with eyes full of serenity. He always seemed to be a little distracted, and he suffered from a constant trembling in his left shoulder. He had studied in Paris, where he found the works of Allan Kardec, the father of Spiritism, and became interested in Spiritism himself. When he went back to Mexico, he began to practice automatic writing as a medium. The Ouija board told him that one day he would be Mexico's president. Despite being a member of one of the richest families, Madero had great social awareness. In his haciendas, he talked to his workers, learned their names, and introduced novel farming techniques that increased the land's productivity. He practiced a rigid body discipline, which meant no alcohol, no tobacco, and no meat, and he encouraged his workers to avoid alcoholism. "My friends," he said to them, "pulque is the dictatorship's best ally, because it degrades and brutalizes the people and delivers them tied, by their hands and feet, to their executioners." Filled with humanistic and philanthropic sentiments, Panchito (a nickname Francisco had, which was a loving reference to his short height) increased the wages of his workers, provided them with medical care, and introduced education to his estates, turning them into productive model units.

Considered as the black sheep of the family, all of whom had good relations with the regime and little desire to get into trouble with the government, Francisco Madero began his career as a writer in two very different genres: as a spiritualist with the nom de plume of BHIMA, and for mundane and more temporal affairs with his birth name. He took his activity as a medium very seriously; he was convinced that he could communicate with a younger brother of his who had died as a child, as well as with another deceased member of his family named José, who told Francisco that he would have to further practice self-discipline because he was going to be entrusted with a mission for the good of the country. Francisco retired to the solitude of the fields, where he fasted and went into a trance, while his father and brothers scratched their heads and thought he had gone crazy. But Madero was sure of his mission, and to him, the Díaz-Creelman interview was like an epiphany.

"A great burden weighs on your shoulders," the spirit of his brother José told Francisco in June 1908, according to the surviving journals written by Madero himself. "You have accepted a momentous mission. This year is going to become the base of your political career, since the book that you are going to write will be the standard that your citizens should judge you with; it will be the measure that will delineate you full-length, the one that reveals to the Union who you are, what your ideals, your aspirations, your aptitudes and your means of combat are." In 1909, Madero finally published his gospel, a book called *The Presidential Succession of 1910.* In its pages, he criticized the concentration of power in one man, absolutism, and the lack of democracy. He criticized the consequences of land dispossession and its concentration in the hands of the few, as well as the alcoholism among farmworkers, illiteracy, and the repression of the nonconformists, but Madero dared not criticize the system itself. His book established the need for a legal-political framework that guaranteed freedom for the citizens and stated that this framework should be respected by the president. It was, in this sense, a cautious and conservative book—it did not talk about revolutions. Madero also took care not to attack Díaz personally; he only wondered what would happen after his death, which everyone was expecting, if the roads to democracy were not opened.

"Dear brother," his beloved spirits disclosed to Madero in his journal entry corresponding to October 27th, 1908, "you cannot imagine the effect that your book will produce in the Republic, especially when the electoral work begins in Coahuila, and take them [sic] to the capital for the organization of the democratic party, which should be accelerated as much as possible, once the electoral campaign begins." The spirits were not mistaken. The book caused a sensation among the political and intellectual elite. Madero's anti-reelection party nominated him to run for the presidency in the 1910 elections against General Porfirio Díaz, who was beginning to dislike that small annoyance of northern Mexico.

1910, the year of the elections, arrived. Madero made a genuine electoral campaign throughout the country, perhaps the first all-out campaign in Mexico's history. He visited several cities where he was already famous. One or two places received him coldly, but he usually gathered crowds. In Guadalajara and Monterrey, the largest cities in Mexico after the capital, more than 10,000 people went to cheer him on, which was an outrageous number, at least for Díaz. Nobody had seen such free-wheeling gatherings in support of anyone other than the president. In Mexico City, Madero gathered 50,000 people electrified by his proposal of effective suffrage and no reelection.

The persecution against Francisco started to materialize through minor issues—a small penalty in money and an investigation for an alleged fraud he never committed in the purchase of livestock—and the hostile tide was growing. Fearing for his safety, Francisco's grandfather wrote a letter to President Díaz, asking him to be lenient with his grandson since he had something wrong with his head, as Francisco believed that supernatural beings were guiding him.

In this caustic letter, Evaristo Madero told Díaz: "No one like you can understand, my distinguished friend, from the experience you have, and the long years you have lived, that in a large family it is common for some member to have extravagant ideas." Díaz did not flinch because he had everything under control. The expected elections were held in June. The day was tense, and if Madero had had hopes of achieving democratic change, his dreams were crushed when he was arrested shortly before election day. He was isolated, and no one could see him, even though hundreds of his followers came to the prison to protest on the day of his arrest. On August 21ˢᵗ, the overwhelming triumph of Porfirio Díaz was announced, as he had carried the election with 98 percent of the vote. According to the electoral results, Madero had only obtained 2 percent of the votes.

Positively certain that the hornet's nest that had been stirred up had passed, President Díaz decided to free Madero at the pleas of his family, who reiterated that he was the weird son and that they had never supported his foray into politics. Francisco boarded a train north but did not stop at home. He continued to the United States, where he had friends. He established himself in the city of Saint Louis and, after deep meditation, wrote a plan called the Plan of San Luis de Potosí, named after the city where he had been incarcerated in a diminutive prison cell.

According to the plan, he effectively assumed the provisional presidency of Mexico and called on the country to take up arms on November 20th, a Sunday. Madero, a pacifist, declared the 1910 elections illegal and called for violence, and he summoned the people to rise around him because he saw no other way. It was a bold move, considering that there had been no triumphant rebellion in Mexico for decades. The plan also demanded free and democratic elections, and Madero also mentioned the issue of land dispossession by the haciendas, which would have to offer restitution of some kind. "The time has come," he wrote in prison.

November 20th was also the Feast of Christ the King, the holiday that marks the end of the Catholic liturgical calendar and thus the end of a cycle— a date with apocalyptic overtones, although it is not known if Madero chose that date with metaphysics in his mind. In one of the last communications Madero had with his brother's spirit, he was told, "Your destiny is great; you have a very important mission to fulfill. It is necessary that in all your deeds you are up to the task. An enormous responsibility weighs on you. You have seen, thanks to the spiritual illumination that you receive from us, the abyss where your country is precipitating. You would be a coward if you don't prevent it. You have also seen the path that the country must follow to save itself. Woe to you if by your weakness, your faintness, your lack of energy, you do not guide it courageously along that path." Madero distributed the plan by mail, sent people to speed the insurrection, appointed provisional governors of the states, and asked the people to respond to his call. The die was cast.

Chapter 4 – Victory Comes Too Soon

"Nothing ever happens in Mexico until it happens."

—Porfirio Díaz

November 20th, 1910, arrived. At one point, Francisco considered abandoning everything and boarding a steamer to Argentina, but his spirits—or perhaps his inner voice—did not fail him. On the appointed day, there were uprisings in several parts of Mexico. Such was the impact of the events that, in a country where everything was repressed effectively and silently, the newspapers in the capital were talking about "the seditious" on the front page two days later. There were clashes with the federal forces and destruction of some bridges and telegraph lines here and there. The press also printed false news that Madero had been captured, all to give some assurance of the stability of the government to the citizens, who were rushing to the magazine stands to buy the papers. A week later, the *New York American* published a telegram from General Díaz, who was trying to calm things down. He said that the Mexican people loved peace and would not accept a revolution, that foreigners had nothing to fear, and that there had only been a few riots in four states: Puebla, Durango, Chihuahua, and Tamaulipas.

But Díaz had miscalculated terribly. Mexico was ripe for a revolution. In the northern states, where there was a tradition of independence and rejection of the central government, and where people had easier access to arms via the United States, there was a real popular uprising. The rebellion in Chihuahua was the first to seriously worry the old dictator. One of the rebel leaders was a former bandit who had changed his name and was now going by the moniker of "Pancho Villa." He later said he had changed his name because he killed a federal soldier who had raped his sister.

At the same time, Emiliano Zapata rose in the south. He was similar in many ways and yet different from Villa. Zapata, a tall, tanned, good-looking peasant with deep eyes and a stern expression, gathered a rural army from the plantations and villages of southern Mexico, seized the lands of the haciendas, and began distributing them among the peasants of Anenecuilco, his hometown. Meanwhile, Francisco Madero was still in the United States, following the news with enthusiasm. He tried to cross into Mexico to lead the rebellion, but after a disastrous episode in which he himself tried to lead some rebels to battle, he returned to the United States, waiting for a better occasion to appear.

"Now we can exert a great influence on him," the spirits dictated to Francisco, referring to President Díaz, "because he no longer has his old vigor and his energy has decreased considerably, while the powerful passions that moved him have diminished with the years." But the revolutionaries in northern Mexico were not interested in metaphysical realities, only in earthly ones. The popular armies were made up of workers who could not find employment in the mines, landless peasants, manual workers tired of the mistreatment at the haciendas, small farm owners threatened by large landowners, and hostile cowboys who had lost their freedom of movement. In 1911, the rebels attacked the strategic Ciudad Juárez along the US border, right at the place where the Rio Grande makes a turn north. Across the river was the city of El Paso, Texas.

The revolutionary forces numbered 3,500 men, while the government's defenders were only 675 stunned soldiers who had never expected an uprising of that magnitude. Madero showed his good-natured and pacifist personality for the first time in Ciudad Juárez. He sent a letter to the general defending the plaza, inviting him to suspend hostilities so as not to get into trouble with the United States. The general agreed, but the revolutionary troops under the command of Pancho Villa and Pascual Orozco continued the attack.

There are photographs of Americans watching the Battle of Ciudad Juárez from El Paso. Some are perched on train wagons with spy glasses. A postcard showing a dozen businessmen-looking spectators watching the Battle of Ciudad Juárez reads: "On the roof garden of Hotel Paso del Norte, the only hotel in the world offering its guests a safe, comfortable place to view a Mexican revolution." However, the free show was not as safe as the postcard boasted. Some lost bullets flew into the other country, and the United States complained to Mexican authorities that there were a few wounded citizens.

Revolutionary troops cornered the federal army in downtown Juárez and finally seized the famous city of Paso del Norte. Villa and Orozco went after the enemy leaders who had been captured to shoot them, but Francisco Madero, the compassionate revolutionary, intervened. Before Villa reached the prisoners, Madero helped General Juan Navarro and his officers escape to the United States in order to save their lives. He took them to the border in his own car and crossed the Rio Grande. The incident sparked bitter disagreement between the rebel leaders and the intellectual father of the revolution, but the troops were loyal to Madero, and Villa and Orozco ceased for the time being. The incident was, however, a preview of the dilemmas Madero was about to face.

The *Ypiranga*

The press was loyal to the government, and they described the revolutionaries as dangerous bandits and reported that the situation was under control, but Díaz knew better. The country was on fire, from the north to the south.

At the other end of the country, 12,000 peasants joined Zapata, who seized the haciendas, distributed the land among his peasants, and refused the usual bribes. "Check the colonial titles and take what belongs legitimately to the people." His scope was eminently local. When asked by the authorities whether he was an ally of Madero's— that is, if he had joined the revolution—he simply said he was returning the land to its rightful owners, the ancestral communities of Mexico. Zapata captured his first important city, Cuautla, after a long siege that came to an end when his men poured gasoline in the city's aqueduct, thus creating a curtain of fire that cut through the town.

President Díaz sent his friends to negotiate with the rebels while at the same time sending a bill to Congress prohibiting reelection. He also made Cabinet changes and expanded the military's budget to dominate the rebellion. The "Strong Man of the Americas" only gave up when the president of the United States, William H. Taft, deployed 20,000 soldiers to the border and dispatched several navy ships to the most important Mexican ports. It is possible that by this point, Madero had the support of the United States, and Taft no longer considered Díaz as someone who could guarantee the interests of the US. Díaz's most important minister, Finance Minister José Yves Limantour, spoke frankly with Díaz: "If the internal war continues, the United States will intervene." That day, the old man understood that his days at the National Palace were finally over.

On the night of May 21ˢᵗ, 1911, under the light of a car's headlights, the Treaty of Ciudad Juárez was signed in front of the closed customs, pursuant to which Díaz and the vice president would resign their posts. Secretary of Foreign Relations Francisco León de la Barra would assume the provisional presidency and call for elections, and the revolutionaries would cease hostilities. On May 25ᵗʰ, the dictator resigned before Congress. In his farewell address, he said that the people had showered him with honors, that a group of "millenarian gangs" had rebelled against him, that he did not know of any reason attributable to him that motivated that social event, and that he was resigning in order to avoid further bloodshed. In his grandiloquent style, he claimed, "I hope, gentlemen, that once the passions have subsided, a more thorough assessment will give rise to a correct judgment that will allow me to die bearing, in the depths of my soul, a fair correlation with the affection that I have given to my compatriots all my life." When the speech ended, the deputies applauded loudly and threw cheers for General Díaz. The next day, Francisco León de la Barra, one of Díaz's trusted men, took possession. It wasn't a very revolutionary transition, but Madero had achieved what he wanted.

Ten days after the Treaty of Ciudad Juárez, Díaz took a last walk through the city of Veracruz, located on the Gulf coast, and boarded the *Ypiranga*, a German-registered passenger and cargo steamer, which would take him to Spain. Escorted by the port's military commander, and standing next to his wife, Díaz received an ovation on his walk to the ship, while a dozen pretty young girls threw bunches of roses before the now-retired president. Some of them stepped forward to present the flowers personally. The cream of society went up to Díaz's cabins to say goodbye to the family, and a band played the Mexican national anthem. A middle-aged general with white hair and a gray mustache called Victoriano Huerta hugged Díaz warmly and said that he could always count on the army. Díaz's last words to those left on the pier were, "I shall die in Mexico."

Unaware of these demonstrations of loyalty to Don Porfirio, Madero traveled south to make his epoch-making entrance at the capital as the leader of the triumphant revolution. Early on the morning of June 7th, 1911, the day scheduled to receive Madero, there was an earthquake in Mexico City, where more than fifty people lost their lives. A few hours later, another earthquake was experienced, this time a civil one, for in the midst of extraordinary popular joy, which had not been seen in a long time, Madero entered Mexico City.

He was welcomed as a hero. Geologically and politically, the capital of the republic was shaken to its foundations.

In their desire to see the man who had commanded the most far-reaching movement ever to change the political conditions in Mexico, people formed in solid masses along the railroad, from the suburbs to the colonial station of the national railway. They filled the huge train shed and yards, and they packed both sides of the streets leading from the station to the national palace, a distance of more than a mile. It was with great difficulty that the lines of soldiers were able to preserve a lane down the broad Paseo de la Reforma for the passage of the automobiles that carried the guests. From the time Madero left the patio of the train station to enter the waiting coach, there was not a moment that was not punctuated with cheers. Francisco's dream had been accomplished: he had overthrown Díaz and organized new elections in which he would be the presidential candidate. Naturally.

It had been the "perfect revolution," efficient and with hardly any bloodshed. It had been no more than half a year since November 20th. If the ghosts said something to Francisco in those days, we do not know it because he did not leave a record. But his rival, Díaz, who was much more experienced when it came to the Mexicans, had left with a warning for the compassionate revolutionary: "Madero has unleashed a tiger. Now let us see if he can control it."

President Madero

On May 25th, 1911, a character with smooth manners and the looks of an aristocrat named Francisco León de la Barra, who had served as the secretary of foreign relations in the last years of the Porfiriato, took office as the provisional president. One of his great achievements as foreign minister had been the organization of the first binational meeting between the presidents of Mexico and the United States, Porfirio Díaz and William Taft, in the city of El Paso. The summit had almost ended in tragedy, as the police arrested a man with a gun who had been approaching the podium. He was caught only a few steps away from both presidents, and who knows how history would have unfolded had he succeeded in killing both heads of state. Luckily for Foreign Minister León de la Barra, the meeting ended without incident.

Throughout its history, the Foreign Office has been one of the most important posts in Mexico, as the man responsible for the position had to perform balancing acts between the great powers of the world and deal with its mighty neighbor, the United States. That Díaz chose his foreign secretary as his successor says a lot about what the old soldier considered to be the most important issue in Mexico in the 1910s: foreign policy. In the face of an unstable country, foreign powers were lurking like birds of prey over Mexico's natural resources.

De la Barra, a member of one of the country's wealthiest families, had a long diplomatic career, although he had no political experience. He had met Queen Isabella II of Spain, called "the woman with the sad destiny," and he represented Mexico on the four-hundredth anniversary of the discovery of the Americas. At his inauguration, de la Barra gave a succinct speech. He claimed that his main objective was to reestablish peace, that under no circumstances would he accept being a candidate for the presidency in the new elections that he would oversee, and that he would guarantee the fairness of the democratic process. Francisco Madero congratulated him on his position, and the new president, in turn, congratulated the leader of the revolution for "his patriotic and dignified attitude" in creating a new era of peace and progress. De la Barra also mentioned that the revolutionary troops would have to surrender their weapons and demobilize. Madero began relaying messages to his troops that they should present themselves at the agreed points and hand over their pistols, rifles, and machetes since the federal army was the only legitimate force in Mexico. In southern and northern Mexico, Zapata and Villa must have removed their hats to scratch their disheveled heads. Villa possibly laughed, as he knew better. Zapata must have frowned. Was *that* a revolution?

As the candidate for the presidency for four political parties, Madero presented as his platform on the principle of "No reelection" and promised to carry out reforms to regulate the political party system and the elections, convert the judicial system, strengthen small rural properties, establish equitable taxes, abolish the death penalty, respect the freedom of the press, promote public education, maintain the separation of church and state, and deploy a conciliatory policy to rebuild the country's economy. Not bad, but for the revolutionary peasants in arms, unemployed workers, and impoverished families, it was like applying new paint to a house in ruins. On the other hand, Madero's program was not something that disturbed the establishment; actually, they were all reforms that many of them had been expecting for years. Furthermore, to the satisfaction of the upper class, Francisco, who detested violence and bloodbath, was pressuring his old allies to disarm as soon as possible, those very men who had taken him to the highest position in the nation. And they were not pleased.

When the elections were held, there was only one name in the mind of the country: Madero. Francisco won the presidency with 99.26 percent of the vote. For Mexicans, the short man with the gentle expression and goatee was the David that had faced Goliath and then defeated him. It was an unthinkable feat. The transmission of power was carried out in the Ambassadors Room before the diplomatic representatives of the nations with which Mexico had relations. The ministers of Belgium, China, Norway, Germany, Austria, Hungary, Chile, Japan, Brazil, Britain, Spain, and the United States were all present, among others. The United States ambassador, Henry Lane Wilson, talked to the president on behalf of the diplomatic corps. A day before the ceremony, Madero promised the American correspondent for *New York World* that in three months, there would be complete peace in the country. Then he went out to greet the people on the esplanade. With Madero in power, and Díaz far away on the other side of the Atlantic, spending his last years as a tourist, the revolution had smoothly come to an end. Cabinet members embraced and congratulated each other. There were hugs, patriotic music, and chants of "*Viva!*" Few imagined that the storm had barely started.

Chapter 5 – The Wicked Ambassador

"When Madero first attracted my attention, he was engaged in the business of making incendiary speeches, usually of very little intellectual merit,

before audiences in remote parts of Mexico."

—Henry Lane Wilson, US Ambassador to Mexico

The honeymoon between Madero and the Mexicans did not last. From the outset, he had many fires to extinguish and few hands to do it. Pascual Orozco, one of the northern rebels who had responded to his call in the Plan of San Luis, rebelled in Chihuahua. Despite the fact that Orozco was one of his old supporters, Madero had no choice but to send the army to fight him. Meanwhile, the press mocked him. Knowing his fondness for Spiritism, newspapers called the president the "madman who communicates with the dead." This heckling, though, was the result of the freedom of the press that he himself had established. In the south, Emiliano Zapata and his peasants were desperate, seeing how slowly the one change that interested them most was being approached. This change wasn't the freedom of the press, democracy, peace, or the separation of church and state; all of these were concerns of the intellectuals. His creed and faith made him believe in recovering the communal lands: *Tierra y Libertad*, "Land and Freedom." Madero insisted that he had to observe legal procedures. When Zapata finally got to know Madero in Mexico City, he suffered a great disappointment.

President Madero had heard rumors that Zapata's army was made of "barbarians," but he had also expressed his sincere appreciation for the southern leader's contribution to the triumph of the revolution. Madero received him at his house in Mexico City, and when he asked him about the number of troops under his command, the polite and nervous president told Zapata that he would no longer need his services and that the peasants should surrender their weapons since the revolution had triumphed. Zapata burned with indignation. Trying to remain calm, he said that he didn't trust the old federal Porfirian army, which was still in place and untouched, and he warned the president that they would not surrender until he returned the lands to the peasants.

"No, General," Madero replied. "The time for the weapons has passed; now the fight is going to take place in a different field. The Revolution needs to guarantee order, to be respectful of property." Zapata, sullen and not given to diplomacy, stood up without letting go of the rifle he was carrying, which, according to eyewitnesses, he kept next to his body even during the meal. Zapata nodded toward the gold chain watch that Madero was wearing and asked him, "Look, Mr. Madero: if I, taking advantage of the fact that I am carrying a gun, take your golden watch and keep it to myself, and after a while we meet each other, both armed and with an equal force, would you have the right to demand me to return it to you?" Madero seemed surprised at the question. "Of course, General, and I would even have the right to ask you for compensation for the time you misused it!" he said. Zapata took a step forward. "That's exactly what happened to us in the state of Morelos. A few hacienda owners seized the lands of the communities. My soldiers, the armed peasants and the people sent me to tell you, with all due respect, that the restitution of their lands should be carried out immediately."

Francisco was worried because he knew that Orozco's and Zapata's anger was just, but he had first promised to restore peace. The rebellions in the north and south contributed to the erosion of the presidential authority, but Madero's greatest menace was a sinister character who acted as a lawyer for the big oil companies and, incidentally, was the ambassador of the United States, Henry Lane Wilson. Wilson looked like a cowboy. He was tall and thin and wore an outdated haircut, parted in the middle. He had enormous power because he was the only ambassador in Mexico— the other countries had only "representatives" or envoys—and because of this, he had a great influence on the diplomatic corps. However, his greatest leverage was that he could decide when the United States should intervene militarily in Mexico. On his recommendation, the US Army and Navy could mobilize immediately. Or at least that's what he boasted.

Wilson never hid his dislike for Madero and his longing for the old regime. On one occasion, Wilson referred to Porfirio Díaz's "wisdom, sobriety and patriotism" after he was gone. Wilson saw Mexico as a country in chaos and believed that Madero had opened Pandora's box and was unable to control it. When Ambassador Wilson learned that Pancho Villa had attacked American property in northern Mexico, he threatened Madero with intervention by the United States. Madero responded indignantly that this would be a declaration of war, but the ambassador did not blink. Madero sent General Victoriano Huerta to control Villa. Huerta, the old general who had hugged Díaz on board the *Ypiranga* steamer and had promised him the army's loyalty, hated Villa. As soon as he had him in his hands, he took the first occasion to arrest him and have him shot. Villa was sent blindfolded against an adobe wall and heard the sound of the guns aiming at him. At the last moment, though, Madero's family stepped in. They convinced Huerta to send him to prison in Mexico City instead. Now, Madero was at odds with those who had been his greatest supporters, with the ambassador of the United States, with his own generals, and with the press, which continued to fiercely attack him. With the strikes, rebellions, peasant protests, and the anarchy that everyone thought they saw, observers increasingly came to the idea that Madero could not guarantee stability. Wilson, who represented the interests of the United States, went berserk when Madero ordered that all railroad employees that worked for the Americans must speak Spanish. The ambassador protested so vehemently that he forced Madero to rescind the order.

The worst part was that Madero's presence no longer aroused the same enthusiasm among the middle class because they thought he was being weak with Zapata, infirm with Villa, hesitant with the other rebels, and did not make them go silent with a bullet, as Díaz had done, but negotiated with them. The press called him "the midget Madero" and printed cruel cartoons that mocked his short stature and suggested his diminished masculinity. Finally, in October 1912, Félix Díaz rebelled in Veracruz. Félix had a familiar name to the ears of the people—he was the nephew of President Porfirio Díaz, and the Mexican aristocracy, with Ambassador Wilson leading the ovation, applauded the news, thinking that the old order was going to be restored. He was, after all, Don Porfirio's own blood and a military man as well. Wilson was pleased with what he saw as an imminent change of power favorable to the US.

But the ambassador had calculated badly. Félix Díaz was defeated and sentenced to death. Again, the humanist Madero changed the death penalty to life imprisonment. With this order, he sealed his luck. This time, more implacable and ruthless forces than those he had fought in 1910 were about to engulf him completely.

The Ten Tragic Days

The furious backlash came in February 1913. In the north, concession-owning foreigners were financing rebels like Pascual Orozco, and everywhere, the federal army was resentful. Madero did not yet believe that his generals could plot against him, but at dawn on February 9th, 1913, one of the most brutal and deplorable incidents of the Mexican Revolution and of Mexican history began, an episode known as *La Decena Trágica,* or the Ten Tragic Days, when downtown Mexico City became a battlefield.

It all began when the disgruntled generals revolted, released General Félix Díaz from prison, and organized a coup to depose Madero. The insurrectionists marched to the National Palace, the seat of the presidential power in Mexico—the equivalent of the White House in the United States—and seized the building. Madero was sleeping in Chapultepec Castle, a mile from the capital. They woke up the president early in the morning to inform him that there was a revolt in Mexico City. Francisco knew that he had to make an appearance in the capital to demonstrate that the situation was under control, but he had few troops at his disposal. The military college was in the castle, so he called the young students to escort him along the Paseo de la Reforma avenue to the main square.

Escorted by 300 cadets, who were dressed in their gala uniforms, several members of the Cabinet, and a few friends, Madero took off from the castle toward the National Palace. He rode his horse along Paseo de la Reforma, holding a Mexican flag, among the applause of the astonished people who saw him. More people joined the column, although, at some point, they had to stop due to bullets flying at them, the source of which remains unknown. That moment is remembered in Mexico every February 9th as the March of Loyalty. A series of photographs taken that day by Gerónimo Hernández, who was running alongside the president, shows him on an imposing horse, waving Mexico's flag as he headed to the main square. Francisco is smiling, greeting the people with his hat. He is followed by groups of people who change with each photograph. Besides his ministers, wearing dark suits, ties, and hats, there are peasants, men in overalls, and youths with suspenders, working clothes, and old-fashioned berets. In several photos, an anonymous boy walks in front of the horse, turning his head to look at Madero. In one of the narrow streets downtown, a disheveled man greets the president with a mashed beret that has already seen its best days. Francisco still salutes with his hat.

Madero during the March of Loyalty. Photo by Gerónimo Hernández 1913. Fondo Casasola, INAH, Mexico.

Moments earlier, a loyal general had recovered the National Palace, but behind them came a larger contingent led by rebel general Bernardo Reyes. Both forces clashed in the main square. Pro-Madero general Lauro Villar Ochoa demanded Reyes three times to surrender. The civilian population looked at the scene incredulously, thinking that they would be safe. Reyes threw his horse against Villar to crush him, and at that moment, the fight with machine guns began. Bernardo Reyes fell, pierced, and so did many of the civilians who were watching. The rebels escaped to a fortress and arms warehouse known as *La Ciudadela*, the Citadel, which aggravated the situation instead of making it better, since 27 guns, 8,500 rifles, 100 machine guns, 5,000 howitzers, and twenty million cartridges were stored there and were now at their disposal. Mexico City was about to become a battlefield. When Madero arrived with his contingent at the National Palace, he saw dozens of dead bodies. Many of them were people who had gone to the morning mass.

Ten days of fighting followed. The extra edition of that afternoon's newspaper described the city as a "river of blood." On the first day alone, more than 800 people were killed, most of them civilians. At the headquarters of the presidential seat, Madero put Victoriano Huerta in charge of the defense. Madero's brother warned him that Huerta was going to betray him. Francisco summoned Huerta and questioned him. After seeing what he thought was loyalty in his eyes, Francisco ratified Huerta as a defender of the city. On February 11th, Huerta attacked the Citadel, where the rebels were hiding. But Huerta put his own men directly in the line of fire of the machine guns, and the streets were littered with corpses. It was not a mistake or simply a blunder on Huerta's part; he had made this decision on purpose. The white-haired general, who had hugged Porfirio Díaz on the steamer and had met with his nephew Félix, had secretly allied with the coup leaders. Together, they had agreed to get rid of Madero. While the plotters destroyed the city with grenades to create a terrifying effect and provoke international alarm, Huerta sent his own troops to unknowingly commit suicide in areas previously established with Félix Díaz. No one in the National Palace understood why the besieged resisted, especially since the reinforcements had reached the city.

Each house became a fortress. The women ran from one side of the street to the other to search for food, carrying white sheets like truce flags as they zigzagged between piles of corpses. The United States embassy car rushed by with an American flag, trying to avoid the bullets. Many photographers risked their lives in capturing the events, but thanks to them, we can see exactly what happened in the heart of the city. Hundreds of photos document the level of destruction in the capital: families piled up in the safest room of the house waiting for the bombardment, mountains of corpses cremated in the fields of Balbuena to avoid an epidemic, and women offering the soldiers a drink of water through their windows.

Meanwhile, a friend of the conspirators met with the alarmed diplomatic corps: the United States ambassador, Henry Lane Wilson. At the beginning of the Ten Tragic Days, Wilson had visited Madero to protest against the savagery of the war, and he threatened him with a military intervention in order to protect the foreign residents. As the self-appointed leader of the diplomatic corps, Henry Lane Wilson told the foreign diplomats that they should ask for Madero's resignation, an action that was clearly out of line.

On the sixth day, the ambassador met with the secretary of foreign relations, Pedro Lascuráin, and told him that he had the power to deploy 3,000 to 4,000 US soldiers to Mexico if order was not restored and that the only way to restore the law was if Madero resigned. From that meeting, he returned to the diplomatic corps to report on his conversation with Lascuráin, although he admitted that, with respect to the American troops, he had been boasting. He immediately sent Spain's minister to ask Madero for his resignation. Indignant, Francisco screamed that they had no right to ask him for such a thing and threw him out.

The next step for the US ambassador was to try to convince the Senate—where Porfirio Díaz still had supporters and friends—to ask for Madero's resignation. A group of them agreed to go and talk to the president, while Wilson sent cables to the United States speaking against Madero and in favor of the rebels in the Citadel. He was in a hurry. President Taft had less than one month left in office, and there was a president-elect—Thomas Woodrow Wilson—who sympathized with Madero. It was a well-orchestrated conspiracy, with flyers against the president being printed in the basement of the United States Embassy. As the days progressed, Henry Lane Wilson invited Victoriano Huerta and Félix Díaz to the embassy to decide who would be the new president. They even appointed a Cabinet.

On the last night, Huerta invited Gustavo Madero, Francisco's brother, to have dinner with him. After dinner, he took him to the Citadel, where Gustavo was lynched by the insurrectionists, who plucked his glass eye with the point of their bayonets and began playing with it, throwing it to one another like a ball. Then they mutilated him. Francisco and the vice president were arrested by a general loyal to Huerta and then locked in a room in the National Palace. Huerta asked Henry Lane Wilson what he should do with Madero. "You decide, I hope you send him to a madhouse!" was his answer. So, Huerta assumed he had the go-ahead from the US to do whatever he wanted with the president. Francisco's parents, sisters, and wife Sara applied for asylum at the Japanese Embassy. The Cuban envoy, fearing for the lives of the president and vice president, offered them political asylum, but Huerta had other plans. Francisco's wife, Sara, ventured outside the Japanese Embassy to beg Ambassador Wilson to intercede for his husband. Wilson, from his arrogant heights, replied laconically that he had warned Francisco that this would happen and that her husband was simply paying the consequences for his bad government.

At ten o'clock on the night of February 22nd, while Madero tried to sleep but instead laid in bed, curled up and crying because his mother had informed him that his brother Gustavo had been brutally tortured and murdered, a door opened. A group of soldiers came in and informed the president and vice president that they would be transferred to a prison while their relocation to Cuba was arranged. As they approached the prison, the car transporting Madero kept going and headed for the plains behind the building. The automobile stopped, and the men ordered Francisco to get out of the vehicle. There was a burning flash on the nape of his neck. Under the starry sky, "Maderito," as his friend Pancho Villa used to call him, fell dead on the grass. A warm pool of blood formed under his battered head.

Chapter 6 – Victoriano Huerta

"Honest and decent people don't come near me,

   so I have to govern with the scoundrels."

—Victoriano Huerta

Pancho Villa heard about Madero's murder while in Texas. Shortly before the Tragic Ten Days, he had escaped from prison in Mexico City disguised as a lawyer. He took the train north to seek refuge in El Paso, where he stayed in a hotel under his real name, Doroteo Arango. He kept carrier pigeons in his room to communicate with his allies in Chihuahua, located in northern Mexico. He had returned to civilian life, riding his motorcycle through the streets of El Paso, and in the afternoons, he sat at a bar where he spoke with other exiled Mexicans. Sometimes he would pay a visit to the Elite Confectionery, a store where he would buy ice cream and strawberry sodas. He was an anonymous Mexican in Texas for the time being, but the latest events, the murder of his friend "Maderito," whom he had loved and respected, aroused his fury.

In Mexico City, Ambassador Wilson and Victoriano Huerta—about whom the best thing people could whisper behind his back was that he was a drunkard—tried to give the coup d'état a legal appearance. Before murdering Madero, they forced him to sign his resignation while at the same time promising to respect his life and his family and send them to exile in Cuba. Presidential power passed, by law, to the secretary of foreign relations, Pedro Lascuráin. As president of Mexico, Lascuráin achieved a banal Guinness World Record, which is the only thing he is now remembered for: he had the shortest presidency on record, somewhere between 15 to 45 minutes, depending on the source. It was a symptom of the times. In his brief tenure as president, all he did was appoint Victoriano Huerta as the secretary of the interior and then resign. Thus, automatically, Huerta, the general with the gray mustache, a coat full of medals, and the eternal scowl, became the new strong man. In the Metropolitan Cathedral of Mexico City, the bishop offered a *Te Deum* (a short religious service of thanks), and the well-to-do breathed a sigh of relief.

The humble people went on Monday morning to the place where Madero's body had fallen to place stones and make small mounds, a Mexican custom. Others brought branches and flowers. When the coffin with the corpse left the prison, the crowd erupted in "wild screams," according to a newspaper of the time that had no qualms about calling them "people of the lowest social class" and stating that they deserved punishment for such a scandal. From there, Francisco's body was taken to La Piedad Cemetery. More than 2,000 people followed the coffin, screaming proclamations or crying openly. The police had to disperse the crowd. As Easter approached in 1913, people began to murmur that Madero was going to resurrect. His grave looked like a garden because people kept placing flowers and plants on it. Like another king had done nineteen centuries before with another tomb, Huerta ordered guards to be placed on the grave because he feared that the corpse would be stolen on Easter Sunday and that the superstitious would drag the people behind them.

Thanks to the guards, Holy Week passed without incident in Mexico City. But if Huerta had hoped that having Madero six feet underground would put an end to his troubles, he was terribly wrong.

The Astronomer

In his youth, Victoriano Huerta had been one of the best mathematicians and astronomers in Mexico. From a very poor family of indigenous origin, the young José Victoriano had entered the prestigious Heroic Military College on the recommendation of President Benito Juárez, a national hero. There, Huerta proved himself to be one of the best students. At the head of several cartographic expeditions, he made maps of the southern part of the country and had almost gone on an expedition to Japan to observe the transit of Venus in 1874. As a young cadet, Huerta lost the opportunity to study military science in Germany because he preferred to stay home to take care of his sick mother. Instead of meeting the Kaiser, he went to fight other Native Americans like him in Yucatan, where the Mayan Caste War was sweeping the peninsula. Military life in Mexico had hardened him. Huerta was reputed to have committed massacres against the Native Americans, was feared for his cruelty but recognized for his dedication and loyalty to his superiors (which had convinced Madero that he could be trusted), and was a heavy drinker. His adversaries made jokes about his constant drunkenness. By the time he became president, his vice had reached alarming levels.

Some saw in Huerta a tough and cruel person, but others saw a strong man, a replica of Don Porfirio. To those people, Huerta was someone who could guarantee peace in a country that was coming apart like a house in flames and shattering international confidence in Mexico, with the consequent drop in the share prices of large companies. On the other hand, with a president like Victoriano Huerta, the promise of real change could be ruled out. The poverty of the working classes, the dispossession of land, the semi-slavery on the haciendas, and the hunger of most of the country's population remained painful realities. For now, Huerta found the national treasury empty, and there wasn't much he could do. He wanted to rebuild the country's infrastructure, and he tried to get loans from abroad, especially from France and Great Britain.

In the United States, Woodrow Wilson took office in March 1914, and in regards to Mexico, he demonstrated that he was not sympathetic to Huerta. In his opinion, he was a usurper. When President Wilson learned from an investigating commission what his ambassador in Mexico had done during the Ten Tragic Days, he was shocked and immediately removed him from his post. Certainly, his antipathy toward Huerta was also fueled by the fact that the Mexican president was in deals with Europe, specifically with a hostile Germany.

President Wilson pressured France and Britain not to grant credits to Mexico. Germany did not abandon Huerta, in part because it was doing the same thing it had done in several peripheral countries: financing movements hostile to its enemies in the face of the impending global conflagration. The German ambassador had offered ammunition and weapons to Mexico on the condition that it stop selling oil to Britain in the event of war. Huerta agreed. In 1914, the *Ypiranga* steamer—the same German ship that had taken Porfirio Díaz to exile—left Germany for the port of Veracruz with a large shipment of weapons for the man with the perpetual scowl.

The American Invasion

In April 1914, the United States sent warships to the Gulf of Mexico to capture the city of Veracruz, the most important port in Mexico. At the head of the expedition was Admiral Frank Fletcher. His orders were to seize the customs of Veracruz and prevent the weapons from entering the country. At eleven o'clock in the morning, 800 Marines made headway to the port in boats. Defending the city was an old general called Gustavo Maass.

A few minutes before, a soldier had approached Maas to tell him that he had a call from the United States Consulate. He took the phone. The secretary of the US Consulate informed him, on behalf of the United States consul, that Admiral Frank Fletcher had orders to disembark and take the port and that Fletcher hoped there would be no resistance and bloodshed could be avoided. The minor-league bureaucrat added that General Maass should remain in his barracks and take no action when Fletcher took the trains and rolling stock at the station.

Maass barked that he could not consent to the landing and that, with the elements at his disposal, he would repel any aggression against national sovereignty. Regarding the trains, he roared that he would do what he considered most convenient. The consul's secretary repeated his orders mechanically, and Maass, after reiterating his decision not to allow the landing, hung up the phone. When he ended the call, his men warned him that the American troops were already at the docks and carrying out the landing in front of the train station. Only ten minutes had passed between the call and the landing.

According to his own report, Maass prepared to receive the invaders with heavy fire. The Americans, who possibly did not expect resistance, returned to their ships under a rain of shrapnel only to return a few moments later with all their force. Maass called Mexico City for instructions. Huerta, who wanted to avoid an open confrontation with the United States, ordered him to retreat ten miles inland. Before withdrawing, the 64-year-old general opened the jails. The army moved inland, but the students of the naval school organized the defense: they improvised barricades, and each cadet received 250 cartridges. Together with the prisoners and inhabitants of Veracruz, who went up to the rooftops with pistols, they prepared to defend the city. The fighting began at one o'clock in the afternoon.

Fletcher was a humanitarian who did not want to destroy the beautiful town of Veracruz, the oldest city in continental America, with its colonial churches, porticoes, cobbled streets, and houses full of flowers. On the third day, the far superior US forces captured the city and stationed there. Their intention was not to invade Mexico but to weaken the Huerta regime by cutting off its main source of income (the Veracruz customs) and, more importantly, impede its trade with Germany.

Despite the fact that many Mexicans viewed Huerta as "the jackal," throughout the country, the people rallied against the invasion. When President Wilson learned that Mexican civilians had resisted the occupation, which had resulted in the death of nineteen Americans and several hundred Mexicans, he was dismayed. In several parts of Mexico, many volunteers showed up to resist what they thought was a new war of conquest. Huerta tried to take advantage of that momentum, but it was not enough. He was fenced on all sides. The blockade of Veracruz benefited a new revolutionary chief and a friend of Madero's, Venustiano Carranza, the governor of Coahuila. After the assassination of the previous president, Carranza had issued his own Plan of Guadalupe to continue the Mexican Revolution. His proclamation was direct and brief. He declared that Huerta's government was illegitimate, as well as the legislative and judicial powers and the state governments. Carranza also expressed his intention to take command of an army, capture Mexico City, assume the presidency provisionally, and call for new elections.

Like the late Francisco Madero, Carranza was a northerner, a landowner, and a member of the upper class. He was 55 years old when he started his uprising. He was spirited and vigorous, but he wore a huge fluffy white beard and small round spectacles that made him look like an old Mexican Santa Claus. Pancho Villa called him goat-bearded. However, Carranza had such determination and energy that, in a short time, he gathered a big army and formed a true opposition against Huerta. Furthermore, Carranza attracted the interest of the United States. With more and more killings, repression, arrests, and forced conscription, even the skeptics were convinced that Victoriano Huerta had to go. "I will not recognize a government of butchers," President Wilson confided privately to a friend in May 1913.

Chapter 7 – Two Hurricanes

—When the Revolution is won, will you be the army?

—When the Revolution is won, there will be no more army. The men are sick of armies.

Journalist John Reed, interviewing revolutionary guerrillas

One of the most compelling metaphors to describe what happened next in the Mexican Revolution is that of a great wind that swept Mexico. With the exception of the two peninsulas in the east and west of the territory—Baja California and Yucatan, where the war barely touched people's lives—there was no place in the country to hide from the dust clouds raised by the warhorses, the gunshots of massive executions on both sides, the laments of a mother who had just seen her daughter abducted by the troops, or the wild screams of the soldiers plundering yet another town. President Huerta tried to negotiate with each revolutionary independently and sent envoys to ask them to lay down their arms. No one accepted. Thus began the most destructive stage of the Mexican Revolution. All of Mexico felt the birth pangs of a new nation that was still far from being born.

Thirsty for revenge after learning of Madero's death, and encouraged by his ideal of justice, Pancho Villa crossed the border back into Mexico on a rainy night in March of 1913. "That night," he later recorded, "I had eight men with me, we had no definite plan, but had decided to make for my old haunts in the Sierra Madre mountains, where I knew that I could find men to follow me. We had one sack of flour, two small packages of coffee and some salt." Villa and his men started ambushing Huerta's army, trying to get ammo and guns. "I told my men that the enemy had those things, and we must take them from him." Villa heard of Carranza's Plan of Guadalupe and joined the cause...for the moment.

By the following week, a hundred men were with him. A few months later, his popular army amounted to more than 18,000 troops, 30 cannons, and several machine guns. First, Villa conquered the state of Chihuahua, which was connected to the United States by train. Battle after battle, Villa took control of all of northern Mexico. He was ruthless with his prisoners of war, whose lives he only spared occasionally when his lieutenant, Felipe Ángeles, intervened, but he also showed a social consciousness. In 1913, he was the governor of Chihuahua for two months. In those eight weeks, he expropriated the property of the rich, confiscated gold from the banks, and established heavy taxes on the upper class; in return, he opened several schools, issued laws to protect widows and orphans, ordered the price of meat, milk, and bread to be lowered, and promised his soldiers and families that he would distribute the lands after their triumph of the Mexican Revolution. Villa set the price of meat at seven cents a pound, milk at five cents a liter, and a large piece of bread at four cents. On Christmas Day, he brought together all the poor of Chihuahua and gave fifteen pesos to each one. He sent his soldiers to patrol the streets, warning them that he would shoot anyone who got drunk or burglarized. There was no hunger in Chihuahua, and Villa became known as the "Friend of the Poor."

Contrary to the popular image of an uncontrolled man, Villa abhorred alcohol and vice. One of the first things he did after taking a city was to pour hundreds of liters of alcohol through the streets to keep his soldiers from falling into temptation. Governor Villa wasn't interested in exercising power behind a desk. In January 1914, he left the governorship, and two months later, he began his march south to

Mexico City, where Huerta was still sitting on the presidential chair. Meanwhile, his army, the famous Division of the North, attracted more volunteers. His conquests were unstoppable, and other generals of the Mexican Revolution began to see him with distrust and uneasiness. The men that followed Villa felt a mixture of admiration and fear, but they were encouraged by his willingness to reward those who were loyal. Legends were woven around the "Centaur of the North," as he was now called, and fantastic tales were told about his exploits.

John Reed, an American journalist who became a friend of Villa's, is one of our best sources for those days when the Centaur was the most popular man of Mexico and his Division of the North the most formidable army. On the field, Villa had to invent an entirely original method of warfare, which involved secrecy, quickness of movement, and the adaptation of his plans to the character of the country and of his soldiers. He established intimate relations with the rank and file, and he built up a superstitious belief among the enemy that his army was invincible and that Villa himself possessed a kind of talisman that made him immortal. He shot enemy officers immediately but spared the common soldiers and invited them to join the Division of the North.

John Reed was intimate with Villa. The Centaur of the North called him "Juanito," or Johnny. Reed observed how, when Villa's army went into battle, it was not hampered by salutes, trigonometrical calculations of the trajectories of projectiles, theories of the percentage of hits in a thousand rounds of rifle fire, or the function of cavalry, infantry, and artillery in any particular position. Villa did not know about those things, but he knew that his men could not be driven blindly in platoons around the field in perfect step because they were fighting individually and of their own free will. Reed thought they were braver than the old-fashioned federal army, whose men had been press-ganged. The journalist, surprised, saw how, when the revolutionaries rushed the streets of an ambushed town, Villa was among them like any common soldier.

Like the Northern Division, other armies during the Mexican Revolution brought hundreds of women soldiers and children with them. There are numerous historic photographs of women, some of them almost teenagers, shooting rifles. "Villa," wrote Reed, who witnessed the Division of the North in action, was "the first man to think of swift forced marches of bodies of cavalry, leaving their women behind. Up to his time no Mexican army had ever abandoned its base; it had always stuck closely to the railroad and the supply trains. But Villa struck terror into the enemy by abandoning his trains and throwing his entire effective army upon the field, as he did at Gómez Palacio [Durango, northern Mexico]. He invented in Mexico that most demoralizing form of battle—the night attack."

In the United States, his exploits were legendary. The Centaur of the North, whose main bases were close to the US border, was a practical man. He affirmed that he was a friend of the Americans. For a time, he was a kind of Mexican Robin Hood, whose adventures Hollywood wanted to glamorize. One of the strangest moments of the Mexican Revolution was when, in 1914, Villa reached an agreement with a film company, Mutual, to film his battles in order to make a movie so the American public would know the deeds of the famous general. Mutual Film Company made him wear a special uniform to make him look more lovable for the camera. "Is Villa a bandit or soldier, a Jesse James or a George Washington, a Robin Hood or a Napoleon, a robber, or a patriot and a hero?" asked *Reel Life* magazine in 1914, and then gave the answer: "Mutual cameramen, who have spent weeks in the field and who have come to know him well, declare that he is a misunderstood and much maligned man."

Mutual Film Company was granted exclusive rights to film Villa's troops in battle, and Villa would receive 20 percent of all revenues that the films produced. However, the footage was not good enough for the director, so Mutual decided to produce a new film from scratch. *The Life of General Villa*, duly sweetened for North American audiences, was released in May 1914 without much fanfare.

Zapata

If there was a Centaur in the north, then there was an Attila in the south. That's the moniker that the virulent press of Mexico City gave to Emiliano Zapata, the peasant leader who fought for "Land and Freedom" for the rural workers.

His agenda was limited but clear. With the stubbornness of a rock, he defended it, unimpressed by promises of economic reforms or political freedom. The land came first, and there was no need to wait. Everything else would come in time. Zapata's peasants in arms were especially hated and feared in the capital. The press called them barbarians, savages from the mountain, and even polygamists. Ordinary people, based on what the newspapers fed them, believed that when Zapata's hordes reached the city, they would kill all the inhabitants and destroy civilization, especially when Zapata, the general with the huge sombrero and mustache, sent a war communique to Mexico City that read as the following:

> At a council of war, it has been resolved to take Mexico City by fire and sword. Drastic justice will be done to all enemies, those responsible for criminal offenses will be executed by the military authorities. The property of the sentenced will be confiscated and sent for the support of the army. All the officers and commanders of the so-called federal army will be executed without a trial, since they are the only ones sustaining the usurper. Should they surrender before they are captured, and are not guilty of other crimes, they will be pardoned. The traitors Huerta and Blanquet will be degraded after a short trial and hanged from the balconies of the National Palace as a general warning. The remaining members of the cabinet will be shot following a summary trial. The lives and interests of foreigners will be respected if they are neutral. Five days will be given to the inhabitants of Mexico City who wish to avoid the horrors of war and [wish to] leave the city.
>
> Signed — EMILIANO ZAPATA.

Every president, from Madero to de la Barra to Huerta, had placed great emphasis on destroying the most radical wing of the Mexican Revolution represented by Zapata. Huerta was particularly brutal, punishing the civilian population of the towns that supported or hid Zapatistas. Entire villages were burned. A witness of the time left a vivid description of Zapata's men and women:

> They were a revolving peasant army, based on their own homes. The soldiers went back from time to time to look after their corn and chili patches. A detachment could, if in an inconvenient military spot, simply evaporate, each man becoming again a soft-eyed, vague-talking peasant by just slipping off his cartridge belt and putting it with his gun in a cache. It was impossible to defeat them, difficult even to find them, as they materialized only when they were ready to attack; and knew, besides, all the shortcuts in their mountain country. They wore ordinary peasant white, except the chiefs who dressed in ranchero clothes; in Zapata's case, symbolic, theatrical, dead-black, skintight and set off with startling silver. The first act on raiding a hacienda or municipal center was sharp and symbolic: they got to the safe and destroyed all papers dealing with land titles, and then invited the neighborhood peasants to homestead on the hacienda lands.

In any case, the loyalty that Zapata aroused among his men was as intense or perhaps more than that of Villa. Both generals were advancing toward the center of Mexico, to the country's capital, where the two titans would meet.

The Battle of Zacatecas: The Deadly Blow to Huerta

The fall of Victoriano Huerta was a direct consequence of Pancho Villa's victories and his Division of the North. The articles by John Reed, who later went on to write a famous book on the Russian Revolution, are invaluable firsthand materials to help one appreciate the drawing power and near-mythical status of Villa during his moments of glory in 1914. It was "the most satisfying moment of my life," Reed wrote as he advanced with the largest army in Mexico toward the capital. He was not a reporter in the traditional sense. He became part of the lives of the revolutionary men and women in order to see the conflict from their point of view. Reed took sides with them to experience the promise of a free nation where there would be no underclass, oppressive army, or dictators.

Reed witnessed how people worshiped Villa even when he was not around. The soldiers composed *corridos* to the Centaur of the North—a musical genre, or war songs of the Mexican Revolution. Next to a fire, the reporter was delighted as a man began to sing a verse from "Francisco Villa's morning song," and then the man next to him composed the following on the spot. Each one contributed to a dramatic tale of the general's exploits for more than three hours.

> Your tamer has arrived, Pancho Villa the fighter, to kick you out of Torreón and to remove even your skin!
>
> The rich with their money, they got a good blow from the soldiers of Urbina and those of Maclovio Herrera too.
>
> Fly, fly, little dove, fly over the meadows, tell everybody that Villa has come to make them run.
>
> Ambition will be ruined, and justice will win, as Villa came to Torreón to punish the greedy.
>
> Fly, fly, golden eagle, take these laurels to Villa, for he has come to conquer Bravo and his colonels.
>
> Now beware, sons of the mosquito, Villa has arrived in Torreón, to deal with the evil deeds of all those damned baldies [the federal soldiers].
>
> Long live Villa and his soldiers! Long live Herrera and his people! Now you know, wicked people, what a brave man can do.

Other famous *corridos* among the Division of the North, such as "La Adelita" and "La Valentina," both tales about women, were preserved and recorded multiple times.

If Adelita left with another man
I would follow her by land and by sea.
If by sea, on a warship

If by land, on a military train.

"La Valentina" is a love song for a young woman showing the fatalistic attitude of the Villistas:

If they're going to kill me tomorrow,

let them kill me at once.

When Villa left Chihuahua, he cut the telegraph wires communicating to the north and forbade, on pain of death, that anyone should carry or send news of his departure. He wanted to take the federal army by surprise. The first serious blow to Huerta was the capture of the city of Torreón. Torreón was an essential railway hub where Villa could control important resources. From that point onward, he let the soldiers' wives accompany them on the trains to cook and sometimes to join the fight, which further increased his army. When Villa boarded his trains with his Northern Division, the scene seemed like an exodus. The next target was Zacatecas, the geographic center of Mexico.

Venustiano Carranza, the chief with the white beard and round spectacles, began feeling jealous of Villa's power and popularity. Carranza ordered the Centaur to put himself under the orders of General Álvaro Obregón. Because Carranza knew that Zacatecas was the strategic point of entry to the south, he ordered Villa to withdraw and desist, but the Centaur ignored the orders. On June 23rd, 1914, in what had been one of the richest cities in colonial Mexico, thanks to its gold and silver mines, the decisive battle of the Mexican Revolution began. Rebel troops attacked from all sides with cavalry charges and cannon fire from the hills. Federal soldiers panicked, got rid of their uniforms, and hid in houses, while a few fled south, where fresh revolutionary troops were waiting for them and took them down from both sides of the road. In one of the bloodiest actions, one of the city's defenders blew up an ammunition depot rather than let it fall into Villa's hands. The explosion destroyed an entire block and left hundreds of dead civilians. Altogether, more than 7,000 military and civilian lives were lost in a single day.

In one year, the Mexican Revolution had left Huerta with only a fraction of the country. However, the opposition to Huerta was far from being a unified movement fighting for a common cause. The only thing that united the armies of the south, north, and northwest was their desire to overthrow the dictator. Although the north of Mexico initially presented a united front, disagreements soon separated the leaders, and none of them recognized the other as the leader of the revolution. Each major general had his own political and, in some cases, economic and foreign agendas, which did not necessarily coincide. There only seemed to be a current of sympathy with Pancho Villa and Emiliano Zapata, since both were peasants and represented the radical, popular wing of the revolution. Although Carranza, a high-class landowner, also wanted to overthrow Huerta, he had more conservative plans.

Good-bye to Huerta

The country no longer belonged to Huerta or to the old Porfiristas. For a critical moment, it belonged to no one; it was a house divided and destroyed by forces financed by different interests. In 1914, during the negotiations in Niagara Falls, which took place there in order to avoid war between the United States and Mexico and which involved the intercession of the ABC countries (Argentina, Brazil, and Chile), the representatives agreed to the end of the US occupation of Veracruz with the condition that Huerta give up. The old general could have stayed and allied himself with other powers, but the country was no longer his; it now belonged to a new generation of revolutionary leaders. On July 15th, the president finally resigned before Mexico's Congress and headed to Veracruz to board the German steamer SS *Dresden* that would take him to Europe. Three years earlier, he had escorted Porfirio Díaz to the same place to board another German steamer that disappeared into the Atlantic. Now, he was following the same destiny. But unlike Don Porfirio, Huerta would not go as a tourist to see the pyramids of Egypt and the Champs-Élysées. On the outside, he looked as decrepit as Díaz, but Huerta was not an old man: he was only 64.

When he submitted his resignation to Congress, the dictator delivered an enigmatic message. With his eagle gaze, he reminded the audience that his solemn promise had been to make peace in Mexico, and for this, he had formed an army. He reminded them about the scarcity of resources he had faced and how "a great power on this continent" had supported the rebels. He mentioned the occupation in Veracruz and the agreements they had reached in the Niagara Peace Conference, and he said that his government had dealt a deathblow to an unjust power. "Robust workers will come later with more perfect tools that will annihilate, without a doubt, that power that has caused so much damage and [is responsible for] so many attacks on this continent." The newspapers reproduced Huerta's speech but were puzzled, not knowing what to do with the message. The old president had not even scratched the United States. Possibly, beneath his prophetic tone, there were other plans that were just materializing in his mind. Huerta, whom everyone considered at the time to be no more than a living corpse, still had a plan. He still wanted to save his country.

Chapter 8 – The Convention of Aguascalientes

Besides Villa, Zapata, and Carranza, there were other leaders in the corners of the country. There was Álvaro Obregón, a former chickpea farmer who had assembled his own army made up of the fierce Yaqui of Sonora. Álvaro Obregón, the rising star in 1914, had a peculiar history. He had lost his father as a child, and his family had moved to a swampy coastal area populated mainly by the Mayo people, where the young Álvaro (whose name means "always prudent") grew up in poverty. There, he learned the language of the Mayo and became a staunch defender of Native American rights. As he was growing up, he worked as a mechanic, barber, painter, teacher, door-to-door shoe salesman, and even as a musician. At the age of 26, he finally tried to grow chickpeas and started exporting crops to the US, and he became a prosperous farmer. When he joined the Mexican Revolution in 1912, his most loyal followers were the Mayo and Yaqui of Sonora, whom he had defended so much throughout his life and whose language he spoke. Obregón was athletic and good-looking, with thick eyebrows and a soft gaze. He considered himself a socialist and led the Constitutional Army of the Northwest, in the same region as

Pancho Villa, in support of Carranza. But loyalties could, and often did, shift.

Other chiefs moved separately without responding to anyone. With no president of the republic, no elections on the horizon, and an entire country up in arms, the only thing left was anarchy and chaos. There were so many leaders, each with a different idea of what Mexico should be, and some of them simply abandoned their beliefs to the game of looting, destruction, and endless fighting. The movement started by Francisco Madero in 1910 threatened to disintegrate the country.

Venustiano Carranza, the self-appointed "first chief of the Revolution," considered that it was time to make a truce and sit everyone down to talk. It was for that reason that he called a meeting in the city of Aguascalientes, a neutral territory 100 kilometers (about 62 miles) south of Zacatecas. Aguascalientes was then a quiet city, famous for its hot springs and its exotic public garden dedicated to Saint Mark. Its orchards of figs, pears, peaches, and grapes girded the city like a belt, despite the fact that the town was located on arid land. It was time, said Carranza, to pass from arms to proposals, to define the country they wanted. The Convention of Aguascalientes was a moment of good judgment and hope in the midst of a country that was heading to chaos.

As the troops approached the shining city, which had remained free from the turmoil of the Mexican Revolution, an air of apprehension ran through the streets. The owners of the inns and taverns worked overtime. The only two hotels in the city were sold out even before the trains began to arrive with the delegates. The hostels were converted into barracks, and many wealthy families had to offer accommodation, not without some apprehension, to military personnel, expecting some protection in return. In the homes where there were unmarried girls, their parents hastily sent them out of town. As for the other family treasures—gold, jewelry, silver coins—the inhabitants of Aguascalientes hid them under their ovens or buried them next to a tree in the backyard.

On October 10th, 1914, the city became the nation's military, political, and nervous center when delegates from Villa, Carranza, and other chiefs began arriving at the Morelos Theater, the headquarters of the Convention. In its inaugural session, 115 soldiers were registered for the debate. The entire republic was attentive to what would be said there. But the Zapatistas were missing, and therefore, the assembly was incomplete, like a car without one of its wheels. General Felipe Ángeles, Villa's most trusted military man, asked that the corps extend an invitation to the men from the south, adding that the Division of the North was in a position to make a complete peace in the country because Villa was in agreement with Zapata.

In an unexpected move, when the Convention began its sessions, it declared itself sovereign and was, therefore, the highest authority in the country. This meant that it was self-vested with absolute power and that it would only respond to itself. One of the generals spoke up and set the tone: "We did not come to discuss whether Carranza or Villa should be president. We came to do a government program and we want peace. We want justice! And know it well: we are not afraid of any of the armies." One by one, the representatives of the armed factions walked on stage to sign the flag that Álvaro Obregón, the former chickpea planter, had brought from Mexico City. When they stamped their signature on the cloth, each general, military man, and chief said these words: "Before this flag, for my honor as an armed citizen, I protest to carry out the decisions of this assembly."

General Felipe Ángeles insisted that the Convention was not complete without Zapata's envoys, and he offered to go on an expedition to the south to bring them. "Gentlemen, let's say to Zapata: Redeemer of the peasants, come here, brother, that there are many arms that want to embrace yours." His proposal was echoed with thunderous applause, and the sober general went south in search of the elusive Zapata. None of the three great men of the Mexican Revolution at that time—Villa, Zapata, or Carranza— were present in the audience. Carranza, not quite humbly, had said that his presence could influence the deliberations and therefore would not attend the meeting. Villa was nearby with his army, a few miles away, in the town of Guadalupe. Zapata had said that he would not go unless they accepted his Plan of Ayala without changing an iota of it.

Actually, the chiefs were being too cautious. They knew that treason was lurking around the corner. However, on October 17th, a distinguished guest appeared in the city: Pancho Villa. He was going to sign the Convention's flag. There is only one photograph of the moment. General Villa, well-groomed and spotless in a new suit, is signing with his right hand. Behind him, four other delegates witness the scene. None of them looks at the camera or at Villa. Since the Division of the North was on the outskirts of Aguascalientes, many delegates feared that there would be a violent takeover, but the Centaur signed and departed, respecting the city.

The Zapatistas Make Their Entrance

On October 27th, the most expected guests arrived at the assembly. The Zapatistas went down to Aguascalientes from the southern mountains. Amidst applause, the commission walked in the theater, and thus, the most mature ideological movement joined the discussions. The spirit of national unity excited everyone. The Convention was, from that moment on, the most authoritative institution of the Mexican Revolution. The Zapatista delegation was made up of seasoned intellectuals with a defined ideological stance. "We regret this division existing among those of us who rose together in 1910 to overthrow a dictatorship that we believed to be invincible," began Paulino Martínez, the leader of the Zapatista delegation, a small man with a formidable mustache who had been an opposition journalist from the Porfirio Díaz era. "We sincerely deplore that our comrades today are perhaps going to be the enemies that we'll fight tomorrow. We do not want this fratricidal struggle." And then, he presented the content of the Plan of Ayala.

> *Tierra y Libertad,* land and freedom is what synthesizes our plan for the economic freedom of the Mexican people...not privileges for a certain social group, but political equality and collective well-being for all the inhabitants of the republic; [we

want] a home for each family, a piece of bread for each destitute person, a light for each brain in the school-farms that the Revolution will establish after the victory, and land for all, because the extension of the Mexican territory can comfortably house ninety to one hundred million inhabitants.

The crowd erupted in applause.

The next Zapatista speaker, Antonio Díaz Soto y Gama, an incendiary orator, walked to the podium and, in mid-speech, grabbed the Mexican flag that everyone had signed with one quick movement. To everyone's surprise, he squeezed it contemptuously and said he would never sign that flag that had waved in the sumptuous buildings of the tyrants. "The word of honor is worth more than a signature," he snapped. More than 200 pistols came out of their holsters, and for a moment, the tension reached unfathomable levels. Soto y Gama stood there without flinching, unmoved. A few women in the upper floor passed out. Desperate, the president of the Convention urged everyone to calm down, reminding them that one shot would be enough to ruin what was being accomplished there. An eyewitness later recalled how people from the upper floors (civilians) rushed to the exit, screaming, pushing each other, and rolling down the stairs, but they were stopped at the entrance by the guards.

A few days after the flag incident, a movie about the Mexican Revolution was shown at the theater. Many Conventionists were amazed because it was the first time in their lives that they had seen a movie. The columns of Yaqui soldiers appeared, then a sequence of General Álvaro Obregón (who was present in the audience), and trains, while the public gaped at the human figures made of shadow and light. The movie seemed so real that when Venustiano Carranza on horseback appeared on the screen for the hundredth time, solemn and expressionless as he entered Mexico City, some shouted, "Death to Carranza!" took out their pistols, and shot the screen. The anecdote was narrated by the Mexican novelist Martín Luis Guzmán, who was also present. Being a civilian, he had slipped through the back door with a friend and sat behind the screen, so they were watching the movie from the other side of the cloth. The bullets landed directly on Carranza's chest and passed just above their heads. "If Carranza had entered Mexico City on foot," Guzmán wrote, "the bullets would have been for us."

The next resolution of the Convention caught the three great leaders by surprise: the delegates asked Carranza, Villa, and Zapata to relinquish command of their respective armies, which were holding the country captive. From Mexico City, Carranza telegraphed that he would resign as the First Chief only if Pancho Villa renounced his Northern Division first and retired into private life. Carranza could not tolerate Villa's independence and autonomy, the strength of his army, the radical social reforms that he had launched in Chihuahua, and the fact that Villa publicly opposed his foreign policy. When he heard that Carranza would resign if he did so as well, the Centaur sent a remarkable counterproposal: "I propose that both of us, the goat-bearded and I, be shot!"

Chapter 9 – The Presidential Chair

The Aguascalientes Convention was, for a few weeks, pregnant with hope, a first parliamentary school in the new Mexico. Since the times of the Congress that had drafted the Constitution of 1857, there had not been an unrestricted and open debate because Porfirio Díaz had had a Congress filled with puppets. But the assembly was not yet over when the armies had moved on to their business again. They had guns at their disposal, and the temptation to use them was great. In the north, General Maclovio Herrera rebelled against Pancho Villa. "That big-eared scoundrel!" Villa thundered. "How could he? I made him! He is my son in arms! How dare that deaf and ungrateful traitor abandon me?" At the Aguascalientes Convention, attempts were made to reconcile interests, but the real politics were something else. The assembly had been divided into two irreconcilable camps, those with Pancho Villa and those with Carranza.

Looking for an intermediate point, the Aguascalientes Convention named a virtual unknown as the president of the republic, General Eulalio Gutiérrez, who, in turn, appointed Villa as the supreme military chief of the new government. It was obvious then who was controlling the deliberations. Cautious, the young ex-farmer Obregón avoided identifying with Carranza. He was sailing where the wind blew. In Mexico City, the chief with the long white beard packed his bags and left for the city of Puebla, having learned of the imminent arrival of the Division of the North. In the south, Zapata's men also began their march toward the capital. They were like two hurricanes that were going to meet in the center. In Mexico City, panic spread because the press depicted the Zapatistas as savages and Zapata as a barbaric and bloodthirsty Attila. Hotels, restaurants, cafés, and drugstores closed their doors, and people locked themselves in their homes. Some students took up arms to defend the city from "the barbarians."

But when the so-called barbarians arrived on November 24th, 1914, the people were stunned. It was a crowd of peasants, most of them indigenous, in white cotton pants, some of them riding starving horses. Some carried machetes, others had rifles, and very few had Remingtons. They covered their heads with large palm hats, wore huaraches, and marched with large numbers of women, some of them very young, almost girls dressed as men, and carrying rifles. Many spoke indigenous languages, not Spanish, and brought banners of the Virgin of Guadalupe. Spontaneously, people started clapping and throwing flowers at them. Contrary to expectations, the Zapatista leaders reestablished order in Mexico City after Carranza's departure, and instead of looting the stores, the men and women went from house to house, knocking on doors and asking for food. A few days later, the Northern Division arrived. General Felipe Ángeles established his headquarters in the Chapultepec Castle, awaiting the advent of General Villa, who arrived by train in early December.

The two great popular leaders, Pancho Villa and Emiliano Zapata, met for the first time in Xochimilco, on the outskirts of Mexico City. They gave each other a warm hug, and the people who witnessed the scene burst into applause, as the north and south were finally meeting. They had both heard of each other. Zapata, who was not much given to express his feelings, understood that Villa, the expropriator of the large estates in Chihuahua, was the only chief who would support his agrarian program. They sat at a table to enjoy a meal consisting of turkey, tamales, and beans with epazote. A secretary who was present at the meal recorded the dialogue between the two leaders for posterity.

Villa: I do not want government positions because I do not know how to "deal" [with bureaucratic matters]. Let's see how we can find these [the right] people. We're just going to warn them not to give us headaches.

Zapata: That's why I warn all these folks to be very careful, otherwise the machete will go down on their heads. (Laughter.) Well, I know that we won't be deceived. We have been limiting ourselves to herd them, to watch them very very closely, to take care of them, and to keep them quiet as well.

Villa: I very well understand that we the ignorant men make the war, and the cabinets take advantage of us; [it's ok] as long as they don't cause us any more trouble.

Zapata: The men who work harder are the least who should enjoy the sidewalks [the luxuries of the city]. I see no more than sidewalks [here]. And I say to myself: when I walk on a sidewalk, I get dizzy and I want to fall.

Villa: This little ranch [Mexico City] is very big for us; it's much better out there [in the fields]. As soon as this is arranged, I'll leave for the Northern campaign. I have a lot to do there. The fight is going to be very hard over there. I'm a man who doesn't like to flatter; but you know, I've been thinking about you for a long time.

Zapata: Likewise. Those who have traveled to the North, the many people who have gone over there, those who have approached you, they must have informed you that I had big hopes on you. Villa is, I said, the only true person, and the war will continue, because as far as I'm concerned, they [the men in power] don't want to make anything right, and I will continue until the day I die.

At the Presidential Chair

Both chiefs agreed that they would enter Mexico City at the same hour and meet at the National Palace on December 6th, 1914. Villa wore a new high-rank uniform, Zapata, a charro suit. There is a film of Villa and Zapata at a banquet that took place at the Palace, but the film lasts for only a few seconds. In the film, one can see, sitting in the middle of them with a suit, tie, and spectacles, the Convention's president, Eulalio Gutiérrez. To his right is Villa, and Zapata is on his left. Zapata, who is visibly the tallest of the three, looks down and eats, leans toward his plate, and touches his face when the camera passes in front of him. Eulalio Gutiérrez moves nervously and gives orders to his assistants; to his right, Villa chews enthusiastically without paying attention to the cameraman, chatting and laughing. The truly iconic moment came later that day when they assembled at the president's office to see the presidential chair. "Is that the chair they fight so much about?" Villa asked mockingly.

A historic photograph of both men at the chair was captured by Agustín Casasola. In it, Villa and Zapata are surrounded by a motley crowd, including some children and a man with a bandaged head. By this point, they were two living legends. The photo is anti-solemn. Villa's laughter, frozen in time, shows that he is delighted. Zapata, who rarely left his southern domains, isn't smiling. "Sit down, my general, please," said Villa, taking off his cap and stretching his arm. "No, you first," said Zapata. "But please, the honor belongs to you," Villa insisted, amused. "No, I'd rather not sit," said Zapata, "because when someone is good and sits on that chair, when he gets up, he is bad."

Villa and Zapata share the presidential chair.
Agustín Casasola, No restrictions, via Wikimedia Commons
https://commons.wikimedia.org/wiki/File:Gral._Urbina,_Gral._Villa,_Gral._Emiliano_Zap
ata._Mexico._12-6-14_(29803803913).jpg

Although Villa and Zapata might have seen the occasion and the ensuing photograph as a souvenir or something to boast about back home, like a hunter with his foot on a dead lion's head, what was happening there was actually unprecedented: for the first time in Mexico's history, the people were in power. The leaders of the revolution had reached their highest point, and they could have ordered whatever they wanted at the moment—the immediate return of the land to the peasants, to improve the workers' conditions, the betterment of the urban classes. But this idea of becoming the person with all the control clashed with the apathy and unwillingness of both leaders, who were more interested in their limited worlds than being presidents of Mexico. Other historians believe that Villa, considering himself an ignorant and unprepared man, was psychologically defeated. Casasola's photo marked the apex of Villa's career and, for that very same reason, the beginning of his decline.

Zapata had never considered living in the city and becoming a bureaucrat, let alone the nation's president. "General Zapata, stretching his face with a kind smile, showed appreciation to the acclamations with slight bows of his head," wrote Francisco Ramírez Plancarte 25 years later in his memoirs, a man who witnessed the historic moment. As Villa and Zapata reviewed the troops from the balcony of the National Palace on the only occasion they met, Zapata's "gaze was peaceful, laying his sweet and vague eyes on the agitated sea of faces." Zapata and Villa would never meet again.

Chapter 10 – Huerta Strikes Back

"Whenever war occurs in any part of the world,

we in Germany sit down and make a plan."

—Kaiser Wilhelm II

"There is vestige of hope in the report that Huerta left his exile in Spain and has gone to America. This strong man could save the country if anybody could."

—*Frankfurten Zeitung*, April 15, 1915

The exiled and overthrown president, Victoriano Huerta, boarded a German steamer to England. From there, he went to Spain. The man with the perpetual scowl arrived in Barcelona in August 1914, three days before the start of the First World War. During the first days of his arrival, tired and in poor health, he dedicated himself to recovering, but he was following the development of the Mexican Revolution with great interest.

In Spain, he came across an elusive German spy and conspirator called Franz von Rintelen, a 38-year-old naval officer whose mission was to open a secret front in Mexico against the United States. "I had studied the foreign political situation in the United States and realized that the only country it should fear was Mexico," Rintelen wrote in his memoirs. "If Mexico attacked, the US would need to use all the ammunition it could make, and it could not export arms to Europe."

Rintelen found Huerta and offered the help of Kaiser Wilhelm II to lead a revolution in Mexico and regain his presidency. Huerta must have smirked and put aside his eternal scowl for a few seconds because he had never once abandoned the idea of returning to Mexico. The fractures among the revolutionaries must have appeared to him as the perfect opportunity to reestablish a strong regime that would have the support of the army and the weary upper and middle classes who were tired of war.

Von Rintelen was serving as the head of the German Secret Service in the US, and he was possibly the most important German spy of the time. In just a few months of his arrival in America, he had successfully exploded fifty Allied ships at sea, staged strikes at American ports, destroyed a New York dock full of weapons bound for Russia, and blown up the Canadian Automobile and Foundry Company. With almost unlimited resources and ample decision-making ability, Rintelen was doing in America what other Germans were doing in the Middle East: fomenting local wars that would distract the resources of the enemy powers. If Mexico were to become a threat to the United States, the US would have to deploy its resources on its own continent and leave Germany alone in Europe. On the other hand, if Germany had an ally in the Americas, it could use Mexico's territory to launch more effective aggression. Ultimately, the Kaiser hoped to convince Mexico to declare war on the United States.

In America, the city of El Paso had become a hotbed of Mexican exiles who, concerned about anarchy in their country and the seemingly endless bloodbath, were conspiring to intervene, take over, and reestablish order. Through an organization called the "Mexican Peace Assembly," they pointed out the excesses of the revolution and compared them to those committed during France's Reign of Terror. At the head of the conspiracy was General Pascual Orozco, who had been one of the first to respond to Francisco Madero's call and was later exiled to the United States. Their dilemma was not only the lack of resources but the lack of a strong figure capable of uniting broad sectors of Mexican society. General Orozco sent Enrique Creel, a member of one of the most powerful families in Mexico during the Porfiriato, to talk with Huerta in Spain.

Creel arrived at the right time, which was one month after the Huerta-Von Rintelen interview. The stars were aligned for Victoriano. The former dictator had accepted German aid, and that same month, he returned to America with Creel in the steamer *López*. In April 1915, when the Mexican Revolution had hit rock-bottom, with the Aguascalientes Convention having failed and the all-out war between Villa and Carranza, Huerta landed in New York, where the press and a handful of enthusiastic admirers rushed to greet him. The man stated that he was on a leisure trip to the United States. Both the representatives of Villa and Carranza in the US protested to the Wilson government for allowing Huerta to disembark in New York, but the old general had his papers in order. In a Manhattan café, the Mexican national anthem was played when they saw that Huerta was there. In the following days, he told the press that a strong man would soon appear to take the reins of destiny in his country, although he did not say who.

For a few weeks, New York became the center of the counter-revolution. Meetings with the German embassy staff were held secretly at the Manhattan Hotel in Broadway, where Huerta met with Rintelen, German Naval Attaché Karl Boy-Ed, and Franz von Papen, a general who had served in the Imperial German Army since he was eighteen and had been sent to organize acts of sabotage in the United States. American intelligence knew about these meetings. Huerta, informed of the Orozco conspiracy and the Peace Assembly, commented to Rintelen that the situation in Mexico was so serious that it defied description, and he requested financing of one million dollars. The agreement was finalized that same month. The Germans deposited almost the whole amount in two bank accounts in Mexico and Cuba, and they promised that German U-boats would deliver weapons to different points on the Mexican coast. It was also stipulated that when Huerta became president again, Germany would support him in both war and peace. On June 1ˢᵗ, 1915, Huerta met with important Mexican exiles at the Holland House hotel. One of them was a spy for Carranza, who telegrammed Mexico that the former president had ten million dollars for his coup, plus the double of that amount in reserve. Finally, Pascual Orozco arrived in Manhattan, finalized details with Huerta, and set June 28ᵗʰ as the date for the invasion.

When the weapons for the conspiracy began to cross into Mexico, the American spies, cognizant of Huerta's footsteps, sent frantic reports to their own government. Two days before the appointed date, Huerta took a train to El Paso, where all the Mexican exiles began to arrive from different parts of the United States. Huerta and General Orozco set the small town of Newman, ten miles north of El Paso, as a meeting point, from where they would ride to Mexico. Everything was ready. At the last minute, Huerta and Orozco were arrested by agents of the US Department of Justice a few blocks away from the Mexican border. "I am now at your orders, gentlemen," said Huerta, without opposing resistance. As the news spread, a crowd gathered outside the El Paso prison, and fearing a diplomatic incident, Huerta was transferred to Fort Bliss. From his compartment in the fort, he sent for help from his alleged protectors. The telegram to Johann von Bernstorff, the German ambassador to the United States, said:

> I am in Fort Bliss and my household consisting of thirty to thirty-five persons who are at the city of El Paso are not accorded guarantees of any kind. I wish to know whether the government of His Imperial Majesty, that you so worthily represent in Washington, can do me the favor of protecting my wife and children as the federal officers of the American Justice in this city do not let them sleep or eat and search my house at will. I respectfully beg your reply.
>
> Victoriano Huerta

Germany ignored Huerta's call for help. In December, Franz von Papen and Karl Boy-Ed were expelled from the United States for conspiracy, and on January 13ᵗʰ, the old general died in his house after several operations without anesthesia at the Fort Bliss hospital. Huerta, who had appeared out of nowhere in the Tragic Ten Days, disappeared from history once again. Had he been successful—and there was a good possibility of this if he had crossed the border—he could have changed the history of the Western Hemisphere. For years, rumors circulated that he was poisoned or killed on the operating table. Victoriano Huerta now rests in a cemetery in El Paso in a humble grave.

Chapter 11 – The Horsemen of the Apocalypse

"I feel it to be my duty to tell them that, if they cannot accommodate their differences and unite for this great purpose within a very short time, this Government will be constrained to decide what means should be employed by the United States in order to help Mexico save herself and serve her people."

—US President Wilson to Villa and Carranza, May 1915

The Aguascalientes Convention came to nothing. The meetings of the assembly moved to Mexico City, but it was not even the shadow of the spirit of 1914. Virtually all of the delegates of Carranza and Villa had withdrawn and were again killing themselves in fields and ravines. In 1915, with an insurmountable wall between the two men, the war spread throughout the country, and the haciendas and cultivated fields were swept away again by the revolution. The country began to resent the effects of five years of war, and famine made itself present. As each faction began printing its own money to cover war expenses, prices went up exorbitantly. Carranza printed banknotes of his provisional government, Villa issued his own money, and Zapata minted coins. According to the region, or the fortune of each general, the bills were either accepted or rejected by the stores.

Given the abundance of worthless paper money, which the populace called "sheets" or "bilimbiques," people returned to bartering. In the days of the most acute inflation in 1915, a worker's day's wages could barely buy a kilo (2.2 pounds) of potatoes. Groups of desperate women stormed the meetings of the Convention with empty baskets. A delegate stood up and proposed to organize a collection to send them away with some money, but the protesters shouted that they wanted bread, not paper. Thinking about how to alleviate hunger, the Convention set up an aid station downtown to distribute corn to the population. When the news broke, thousands of people ran to the Palacio de Minería and flooded the courtyards. There was such chaos that people had to be dispersed with bullets. By mid-1915, groups of women walked the markets with empty baskets, only to find the stores were closed. Some people began tearing down the doors of the shops with axes and sticks, and the store owners defended their properties, shooting from the rooftops. Obregón even threatened to shoot the merchants who hid basic goods.

That same year, a typhoid epidemic struck the center of the country due to malnutrition, lack of personal and environmental hygiene, and poverty. Sometimes people would collapse in the middle of the street, their stomachs empty or their body ravaged by typhoid. The destruction and blockade of roads by the opposing armies, which interrupted the supply of goods to Mexico City, did not help. Every new army that occupied the capital— first Carranza, then Villa and Zapata, then Obregón, then Zapata again—depleted its meager reserves, aggravated the situation, and produced thousands of beggars and orphans in the streets.

The End of the Division of the North

To the relief of many, the most intense period of the civil war came to an end in the year 1915, the "year of hunger," with a massive bloodbath in central Mexico, where Pancho Villa suffered a series of defeats against the rising star, General Álvaro Obregón.

First, Obregón defeated the Zapatistas in Puebla and entered Mexico City. He let his beard grow and said he would not cut it until

Villa was liquidated. Obregón took other cities in the center of the country, getting closer and closer to the Centaur, who also yearned for the final showdown so he could wipe out Obregón's army and then destroy the rest of Carranza's forces. Both titans met in the surroundings of the city of Celaya. The shooting started at four o'clock in the afternoon, and the fighting lasted for the rest of the day and all of the following night. Obregón telegraphed to the venerable-looking Carranza, "The assaults of the enemy are very crude. As long as a soldier and a bullet remain, I will know how to do my duty." At dawn, the Villistas tried again and again, without success, to storm the plaza until Obregón mobilized two powerful groups of cavalry to envelop the attackers from the south and the north. The Division of the North, which had no reserves, withdrew orderly at first and then in complete disarray. "The Villistas have left the field strewn with corpses," Obregón reported.

In the following days, Obregón got reinforcements, and his troops reached 15,000 soldiers. Villa's more experienced generals advised him to avoid the combat and retreat north, as the terrain was uneven and full of trench holes, but Villa still felt invincible. On April 13th, he attacked again, now with greater momentum, looking for a weak point in the defense. The Villistas depleted their force in fruitless assaults, and two days later, when the Centaur had already been fighting for 36 hours, Obregón ordered a counteroffensive. Mexican journalist Anita Brenner, who wrote one of the first histories of the Mexican Revolution in 1938, left a dramatic description of the final battle:

> Against Villa's massive cavalry attacks, Obregon's strategy was to advance very fast, stop at some good fortifiable point, set up barbed wire entanglements and lay out trenches, in open loop shape, in which he put chiefly the Yaqui troops who were the core of his personal army. They had been fighting for generations, trained to win or commit suicide. When the fight began, the Yaquis lay each one in a trench-hole with his wife and children, who kept handing him a reloaded gun as fast as one was finished, and if he was

wounded or killed, they continued firing. Cavalry issued to charge head-on into the Dorados [Villistas], and then to run apparently routed, into the open loop, where the Yaquis caught the pursuing Dorados in murderous crossfire. They massacred the first wave and the second and sometimes a third. The same sort of trap closed on them in battle after battle.

Before retreating like a wounded animal, Villa had one last gift for General Obregón. In the heat of battle, a grenade hit Obregón and blew off his right arm. Seeing himself mutilated like that, the handsome general pulled out his gun to commit suicide, but his weapon was unloaded, as his aide had forgotten to load it that day. Although he was out of combat for a few days, Obregón returned to finish off the invincible Northern Division, as he had promised, in the battles of León and Aguascalientes. There, he obliterated the bulk of Villa's forces and acquired a new nickname: El Manco de Celaya (the one-armed man of Celaya). His amputated hand, which the doctor kept in formalin inside a jar, would go on to have a bizarre adventure. Meanwhile, the former chickpea planter saw his star reach its zenith and finally shaved his beard, while Villa, with the remnants of his army, retreated north in a sad parade. He was not a threat to Carranza anymore.

After Celaya, as rumors grew that Villa had been defeated, that he had become more brutal, and that Germany had approached the Centaur with offers, the United States gave official recognition to Venustiano Carranza's "pre-constitutional government." With somewhat reluctant acceptance, US President Wilson hoped to stop the civil war to the south of the US border. In May 1917, without opposition, Carranza won the presidential election.

Villa was furious, but most of all, he was incredulous. He had always ordered to respect American property, had always had a favorable attitude toward the United States, had made friends with American reporters and filmmakers, and had even looked the other way during the occupation of the port of Veracruz in 1914. "I emphatically declare that I have much to thank Mr. Wilson for," Villa told a reporter, "because this now relieves me of the obligation to give guarantees to foreigners, and especially to those who once were free citizens and are now vassals of an evangelist Philosophy professor. Therefore, I decline all responsibility in the future." His words were a genuine and grim warning.

Chapter 12 – The Centaur and the General: Pershing's Punitive Expedition

Defeated by Obregón's forces, betrayed by the United States, and abandoned by his generals who were deserting him, including the prized general Felipe Ángeles, the architect of his triumphs and moderator of his tantrums, Villa's worst side took possession of him. The man, who has been described as both a compassionate angel and a butcher, had reason to feel like a cornered beast. In early 1916, with Venustiano Carranza in possession of Mexico, Villa was now reduced to a fugitive wandering through northern Mexico in search of provisions; he was no more than a bandit. The newspapers that previously praised him referred to him and his last faithful soldiers (the famous Dorados) as mere desperados.

On January 10th, the Villistas derailed a passenger train that was heading to a mining town called Cusihuiriachi (Cusi, for short). The train was transporting eighteen Americans who had been invited by the Mexican government to reopen some mines. The Villistas boarded the train, shot some of the Americans in cold blood while they were still in their seats, and stole their money. Others were taken off and shot on the spot. Only one American businessman, who played dead, survived and was able to reach Chihuahua to tell about the massacre. When the citizens of El Paso found out what had happened, they were so furious that the authorities had to declare martial law to prevent them from going to kill Mexicans across the river.

Two months later, on March 9th, 1916, at three o'clock in the morning, Villa crossed the border into the United States with 480 soldiers and some prisoners to attack the small town of Columbus, New Mexico. Columbus was a settlement struggling to survive in the middle of the desert. It had a hotel, a bank, a drugstore, a clothing store, a church, about 300 inhabitants, and a railroad track that was its only contact with the bigger world. While Columbus was sleeping, three columns of Villistas penetrated the quiet town, shouting, "Viva México!" and "Viva Villa!" According to some witnesses, they also shouted, "Let's kill the gringos!" The Villistas began shooting into the houses, forcing entry into commercial establishments, and looting. At the hotel, which was on the second floor of a building, the attackers forced the male guests down the stairs and executed them one by one, while the women watched as the corpses formed a pile in the middle of the street. The attackers seized horses, food, mules, clothing, cigarettes, jewelry, and sweets. The sound of machine guns was heard throughout the town, and the fire was so intense that there was a ghostly glow shifting from one position to another. Archibald Frost and his wife Mary Alice, who had a furniture store, hid in their basement, but they later thought better of it and hurried to their garage to look for their car. When Archibald tried to turn on the engine, the Villistas came and shot him, but he managed to get up and escape. Halfway to Deming, he was bleeding so profusely that his wife Mary Alice had to take the wheel. Behind their backs, they saw the glow of the flames consuming the stores and the Commercial Hotel.

After the initial surprise, the inhabitants of Columbus formed barricades and began to defend themselves. The location of Pancho Villa during the attack has been the subject of much discussion. Many say that he stayed on the Mexican side, but Maud Wright, a woman who was being held prisoner with the Mexicans and released in Columbus, claimed that Villa was in the middle of the town, screaming, cheering his troops, and striking the fallen or scared soldiers with his saber in order to send them back to the battle. Although the soldiers at the American camp had suspected that Villa was planning something, they reacted painfully late. By dawn, they managed to repel the attackers and chased them beyond the border. Villa, according to witnesses, took off his hat and shook it defiantly, waving goodbye at the American troops who followed him.

In the United States, outrage struck the country like lightning, and strident voices demanded to intervene militarily. Within days, nearly 10,000 soldiers were stationed along the border with Mexico, and the first warplanes began to fly over the state of Chihuahua. Villa's reasons for attacking an insignificant population and killing innocents in the middle of the night have been hotly debated. According to the Villistas themselves, many of them being interviewed decades later when they were old men, Pancho Villa was outraged because he believed that Carranza had sold the country to make it a protectorate of the United States. Villa had promised his men that they would march to Washington. "The United States wants to swallow Mexico: let's see if they'll choke with it in its throat." In any case, Villa could not have been so naive as to think about invading the American Union, but he could take revenge for what he perceived as treason. Others, like the eminent historian Friedrich Katz, see Germany's hand behind the attack, reasoning that the Kaiser was hoping to provoke a war in North America that would divert US resources. A third explanation has been offered, which is that Villa wanted to punish a Columbus arms dealer who sold him defective weapons and contributed to his resounding defeat in Celaya. The final explanation possibly has a combination of the other two mixed in there. The witnesses insist that the Villistas searched everywhere for the arms dealer named Sam Ravel, who, luckily, was in El Paso. There is a mountain of evidence of Villa's involvement with Germany and of his belief that Carranza had sold out to the United States. In 1975, a letter from the time of the attack on Columbus was discovered by Katz. In it, Villa invites Emiliano Zapata to join forces to invade the United States. The most significant extracts say:

> My projects were frustrated, because the enemy [Carranza] had the undue and shameless support of the American government...the integrity and independence of our country is about to be lost if we, all honest Mexicans, do not unite in arms to prevent the sale of our homeland, and you must already know about the treaties that Carranza agreed with the Washington Government...Since the movement we have to make against the United States can only be carried out [here] in the north, and in view that we do not have ships, I beg you to tell me if you agree to come here with all your troops, on what date, and I will have the pleasure of personally going to meet you, and together we will undertake the work of rebuilding and ennobling Mexico, and punishing our eternal enemy.

The attack on Columbus represents Villa's lowest point, who was an otherwise heroic figure; it achieved nothing and took innocent lives, and it nearly provoked an international war. In the United States, many outraged and opportunistic voices called for a new intervention to punish Mexico, but with World War I going on in Europe, President Woodrow Wilson knew that the path of prudence was of the utmost importance. However, the US approved an expedition under the command of General John J. Pershing and several thousand men to capture Villa. Carranza also sent a large group of men to hunt down the Centaur of the North.

Pershing's army grew to 10,000 men, who were deployed in three columns that included infantry, cavalry, field artillery, and eight airplanes. The American general led his men 700 miles into Mexico through plains so desolate and monotonous that photos of the expedition remind one of those taken by Roald Amundsen in his journey to the South Pole four years earlier. Pershing's first enemies were frequent dust storms, swarms of flies, and boredom among his troops. "Where is Pancho Villa?" asked Pershing in his broken Spanish in each ranch and village in the mountains, only to get misleading or extremely confusing information from villagers. In several parts of the state of Chihuahua, Pershing found bands of Villistas, and fighting ensued in Ciudad Guerrero at the end of March, in Agua Caliente on April 4th, and Parral on April 11th, with the latter having started by the civilian population attacking the Americans. Pershing's incursion increased Villa's waning popularity among northern Mexicans, who gave Pershing the wrong directions when he asked where the bandit was. These events were followed by an urgent exchange of diplomatic notes and then a conference between Generals Hugo L. Scott, the chief of staff of the United States Army, and Álvaro Obregón.

In a skirmish with a Carrancista general, Francisco Bertani, Villa was wounded in the leg by one of his own men, who tried to betray him when he thought Villa was finished. The Centaur fell from his horse, bleeding, but to his good luck, the enemy did not notice. For almost three months, nothing was heard of him, and the newspapers repeated the rumor that he had died. Carranza sent a party to find Pancho Villa's alleged tomb in the mountains, with the help of guides who claimed to know the location of the makeshift grave. But the Centaur was not dead. His men had taken him with infinite difficulties on the back of a donkey to an ultra-secret cave in the mountains, whose whereabouts were known only by a handful of his most faithful companions. They covered the entrance with branches and left him alone, only visiting to bring food. For six weeks, they fed him with a few handfuls of rice and some sugar, while his broken femur healed. The drinking water had to be collected fifteen kilometers (a little over nine miles) away from the cave. His leg swelled, leaking pus, and the Centaur suffered unspeakably.

Carranza, meanwhile, exerted intense diplomatic pressure to bring Pershing's expedition to an end. In the middle of Chihuahua, numerous Mexican troops gathered with the order to stop the

American advance. Pershing was notified but refused to back down. On June 21ᵗ, 1916, the armies met. Captain Charles T. Boyd and Mexican General Félix Uresti exchanged warnings and screamed at one another, then withdrew to prepare for battle. The clash was no longer between Pershing's men and Villistas but between the American and Mexican armies. The skirmish lasted more than three hours and strained the binational relations to the breaking point. The hawks in the United States played the drums of war, and President Wilson sent warships to both Mexican coasts.

In the beginning, the peace conferences stalled because Carranza demanded the withdrawal of the American troops as an absolutely necessary condition, while President Wilson, on the other hand, did not want to appear weak before the Mexican government. Finally, a treaty was signed in which the Punitive Expedition would leave the country. The imminent breakdown of relations between the United States and Germany contributed to the settlement. Villa, meanwhile, remained hidden in a cave in the rugged Sierra Madre.

"I have the honor of informing you," Pershing wrote his report at the end of the day, "that Francisco Villa is everywhere and nowhere." The Punitive Expedition returned to the United States without fulfilling its objective. In private, the famous military leader later admitted that "when the true history is written, it will not be a very inspiring chapter for school children, or even grownups to contemplate. Having dashed into Mexico with the intention of eating the Mexicans raw, we turned back at the first repulse and are now sneaking home under cover, like a whipped cur with its tail between its legs." Pershing was probably too hard on himself. Thanks to the Punitive Expedition, the United States stretched its muscles and implemented new tactics, experimented with new weapons in Mexico (including mechanical vehicles instead of cavalry), and, for the first time, deployed its military aircraft. It was a warm-up for what was coming next year. The American generals received good field training, including a young George S. Patton. Pershing would go on to become

his country's commander of the American Expeditionary Forces on
the Western Front in World War I.

Chapter 13 – The Zimmermann Telegram

In search of legitimacy for his government, Carranza called a Constituent Congress in late 1916 to draft a new constitution. The assembly did not meet in Mexico City but rather in Querétaro, 200 kilometers (almost 125 miles) north of the capital, and it was symbolically chosen for it was the place where the foreign emperor Maximilian of Habsburg was shot. To Carranza's discredit, he did not invite Villistas or Zapatistas, but in an act of poetic justice, many constituents formed a radical and progressive wing—which Carranza had never expected—that incorporated many of Zapata's ideas into the document. It was the legacy of the Convention of Aguascalientes. Many constituents understood that if they did not include progressive reforms, the last seven years of their struggle would have been in vain, and they would be disloyal to thousands and thousands of peasants whose blood had been shed.

The Mexican Constitution was approved on February 5th, 1917, and it was the first in the world to guarantee the social rights of workers and peasants, establishing bases for agrarian reform and empowering the working class. According to the Encyclopedia of World Constitutions, "it can be affirmed that social constitutionalism, or the social democratic rule of law, was modeled by this constitution, and was the inspiration for others, such as the Weimar Constitution of 1919 and the Russian Constitution of 1918." Democracy is not only a political regime but a way of life, founded on constant economic, social, and cultural improvements for the people.

Mexico would have to go a long way to achieve this ideal. The Constitution was only signaling the route they had to take. Meanwhile, the country had the urgent need to end the armed phase of the Mexican Revolution and proceed, as President Plutarco Elías Calles would say a few years later, to a revolution of the minds. In the year of the new Constitution, a puzzling international incident involving Germany, Mexico, and the United States occurred in the final part of the Mexican Revolution, which changed the history of the 20th century. In January of 1917, while the new Constitution was being drafted, the British intelligence service intercepted a telegram sent by German Foreign Secretary Arthur Zimmermann to the German ambassador in Mexico, Heinrich von Eckardt. When the British showed the paper to the US Embassy in London, the Americans thought it was a joke. But once they learned it was authentic, and its content was disseminated in the American press, the American people burned with indignation. In the telegram, Arthur Zimmermann instructed the ambassador to begin negotiations with President Carranza so that, with German support, Mexico could declare war on the US. In return, it would get "generous financial support," and if the Central Powers won World War I, Mexico would recover the states of Texas, New Mexico, and Arizona, the territories it had lost in 1847. The telegram, decoded by the intelligence of Great Britain, said:

> We intend to begin on the first of February unrestricted submarine warfare. We shall endeavor in spite of this to keep the United States of America neutral. In the event of this not succeeding, we make Mexico a proposal of alliance on the following basis: make war together, make peace together, generous financial support and an understanding on our part that Mexico is to reconquer the lost territory in Texas, New

Mexico, and Arizona. The settlement in detail is left to you. You will inform the President of the above most secretly as soon as the outbreak of war with the United States of America is certain, and add the suggestion that he should, on his own initiative, invite Japan to immediate adherence and at the same time mediate between Japan and ourselves. Please call the President's attention to the fact that the ruthless employment of our submarines now offers the prospect of compelling England in a few months to make peace.

Signed, ZIMMERMANN.

Of course, the telegram was only useful if its contents remained secret to the United States and its allies. After being displayed on the front page of every paper in the world, it became practically useless, a skeleton brought out of the closet. If Carranza learned about its contents from the newspaper like everyone else or through his foreign minister, Cándido Aguilar, it is not known, but it is a fact that the president with the long white beard at least considered the possibility to seize the day and get something from Germany.

Carranza sent his foreign minister, Aguilar, to talk with Heinrich von Eckardt, Berlin's envoy in Mexico City, and ask him whether Germany could provide weapons. A few days after the telegram was disclosed, Germany offered, through Captain Ernst von Hülsen, to provide 30,000 rifles, 100 machine guns, six mountain cannons, and four howitzers. This was clearly not enough to declare war on the United States, but it was enough to create a continental distraction. Von Hülsen knew that it would be impossible to send weapons to Mexico due to the British blockade, so he proposed that instead of ships with hardware, Germany should send cash to Carranza so that he could buy the weapons from South America. An amount of thirty million marks was established, and it is not clear whether this money ever changed hands from Berlin to Mexico City.

Carranza also established a commission to investigate whether Mexico should agree to the more serious terms of the telegram—to join the Central Powers and declare war on the Allies. The Germans promised more money and weapons to help wage war on the United States, but most likely, Carranza was simply playing with the Germans, trying to get funds from whatever source he could in order to consolidate his power with minimal commitment. The Mexican president was not the only man to play with both sides of the equation. Eckardt started meeting secretly with other generals to overthrow Carranza. On April 14th, 1917, Carranza finally declined Zimmermann's proposal, but he did not close all the doors. "If Mexico is dragged into the [First] World War in spite of everything, we'll see. For now the alliance has been frustrated, but it will be necessary later on at a certain moment."

Mexico remained a neutral nation, but the Zimmermann Telegram threw the hitherto neutral US into the First World War, and as a result, the United States turned its attention away from Mexico for good. Carranza was thus firmly established in the presidency. Villa was out of sight, without an army, and being persecuted as a bandit. Obregón had retired into private life in his ranch, and Huerta was dead. There remained only one small nuisance: Zapata, who survived in the south, resisting armed incursions, arsons, and bribes—even the Mexican Air Force found its first military use against the Zapatistas. So, Carranza decided to murder him.

Death of Zapata

Like Villa, Zapata was an international celebrity, a combination of a bandit and a popular hero, a peasant with a huge hat that people looked at with a mix of fear and reverence, a man whom his time did not understand. His recognition as a social fighter would only come after his death. His critics saw him as a threat to order and decency. "Zapata seems to belong to some other century," wrote *The New York Times* in early 1919. "Savage, boastful, fond of loading his person with diamonds and gold, polygamous, a patriarch of banditry, he fulfills the book-and-boy idea of a robber." Zapata had never thought in national terms but rather in local ones. So, while Carranza and his armed hand Obregón took care of Pancho Villa, Zapata was free to materialize his social program and distribute land among the peasants in Morelos.

The state of Morelos, Zapata's headquarters, experienced peace for the first time in years. The peasants, now in possession of their land, no longer planted sugar or rice for the haciendas but corn, beans, chickpeas, onions, and chili peppers for their families. Its communities were reborn in that period, according to John Womack, one of Zapata's most distinguished biographers: "They even refused to allow wood to be cut for railway sleepers and fuel, or give permission to draw water for the locomotives. For the harassed officials of Mexico City this was the work of evil and superstitious peasants. But the Morelians understood the question differently: the old contracts with the haciendas and the railroads were no longer valid; wood and water now belonged to them."

The utopia did not last long. Free from Villa, the Carrancistas went to the south with spies and agitators, and in October 1917, they returned once again with soldiers. Throughout 1918, the Zapatistas, the last rebel faction, suffered a relentless hunt by the army. Anita Brenner commented in her history of the revolution, "In the sugar country Zapata held out against the government's general Pablo Gonzalez, who warred by the 'scorched earth' method—he destroyed every village he thought might harbor Zapatistas, killing all the males." Like Villa, Zapata was a fugitive now. He often used a double for meetings. Some of his men, desperate, took amnesty from the government, while others, disappointed and angry, punished the traitors.

Finally, in April 1919, the army ambushed him. Zapata's men told him rumors that a very apt colonel named Jesús Guajardo had broken with Carranza. Zapata calculated that if he had Guajardo on his side, he could strengthen his thinning army. He sent him a letter with an invitation to join his troops. Guajardo had indeed declared himself to be in rebellion and had taken the town of Jonacatepec, where he shot the traitors to Zapata, but his actions were a carefully planned deception. Zapata was warned by his spies of possible treason, but he ignored them. On April 10ᵗʰ, the southern leader came down from the mountains with an escort of thirty men to meet with Guajardo at the Chinameca hacienda.

The general ordered his men to wait outside; he moved inside with ten guards only. In the courtyard, the soldiers formed a line to present arms. A bugle called three times. When the instrument went silent, all of the men in formation opened fire at the same time. Zapata fell. He was dead, there and then. The news brought great joy to the government but tears to the towns of southern Mexico. Carranza promoted Guajardo to division general and gave him a prize of 50,000 pesos in silver coins.

The body was taken on a mule to Cuautla, the capital of the state of Morelos, where it was photographed and exhibited so that people would be convinced that the southern leader had really died. The prevailing feeling among the common folk was disbelief. Zapata was only 39. One of the few existing photographs of Zapata's corpse when it was on display in the Cuautla main square shows him in his white shirt completely darkened with blood. His expression is peaceful as if he were asleep. His body broken, Zapata lies in the lap of four men— Zapatistas probably—whose expressions are similar to those of saints in a mystical rapture. One of them looks away at the sky, another's chin rests on Zapata's hair, a third reclines his left side on the leader's forehead, and the fourth peasant, with intense indigenous features, looks at the camera with an expression of indignation. Two days later, Zapata was buried in the Cuautla cemetery. According to a reporter who was covering the story, when the funeral procession arrived, there was an unknown elderly woman waiting by the grave, on her knees. The undertakers lowered the coffin, but before they dumped the earth, the woman stood up, took some dust, and threw it on the casket. Then she withdrew, wiping away her tears with the tip of her shawl—a perfect metaphor for the state in which those communities were left.

Zapata's blood-soaked clothes were displayed in a street of Mexico City, outside the premises of a newspaper. Many in Morelos did not buy it; they said that it was, in fact, his double who had been killed, as the body had a scar missing, and the fingers of the corpse were shorter. For many years, even until the 1940s, people in the southern mountains claimed to have seen Zapata on his horse.

Emiliano Zapata dead. Unknown photographer, 1919.
Originally published in the newspaper Excelsior, Mexico.
https://commons.wikimedia.org/wiki/File:El_cad%C3%A1ver_de_Emiliano_Zapata,_exhibid o_en_Cuautla,_Morelos.jpg

Carranza, now satisfied, had no idea that he would join Zapata in the grave the following year. In 1920, the year of the presidential election, he proposed a civilian as a candidate for the presidency, a virtual unknown surnamed Bonillas. This apparently was the pretext for a group of generals from the north to join a rebellion to remove

Carranza. A popular general came to the fore: Álvaro Obregón, who, besides planting more chickpeas, had been meditating on his political ambitions. The rebellion against Carranza, the latest in a long series of ten years, caught like fire on dry grass. In May 1920, the patriarch left the capital with the national treasury bound for Veracruz, as he had once done before, but his time had come. His train derailed, and Carranza dismounted with his most trusted men and continued on horseback, passing some ranches, crossing a river, and finally reaching a place called Tlaxcalantongo. On the night of May 21st, 1920, while sleeping in a hut, a group of traitors on horseback rushed over to his cabin. "Licenciado [lawyer], they broke my leg!" were his last words. The man with the long white beard was dead. In the official story, the traitors killed him, but more recent opinions, based on analysis of his clothes, say that Carranza preferred suicide rather than see himself in the hands of his enemies.

With his death, a cycle was closed. Currently, Carranza was the last president of Mexico to be overthrown or to be unable to finish his term, a fate that practically all of the presidents of Mexico in the last one hundred years before him had gone through. He was also the only president to be killed during his tenure. On December 1st, 1920, exactly ten years after the beginning of the Mexican Revolution—minus ten days—the last player on the field, Álvaro Obregón, assumed the presidency of the republic. Possibly the most skillful general in Mexico's history, Obregón had won all his battles and had finally emerged as the victor in the longest war of his country. And he had only lost one arm.

Chapter 14 – Aftermath

After a decade of fighting and between one and three million deaths (the figure is still disputed), the Mexican Revolution, which had initially started to restore democracy and then to regenerate the country's economy, proved to be the most expensive war and with more casualties in Mexico's history. But the long struggle did raise awareness of the need for social justice, starting with land distribution, labor reform, and education for the people. The ideals promoted by fighters such as Madero, Villa, and especially Zapata were embodied in the new Constitution promulgated in 1917, which still governs the land today.

The Mexican Revolution, a decisive event in the formation of 20th-century Mexico's philosophy, economy, and even artistic development, was, in the words of distinguished historian Alan Knight, one of those "relatively rare episodes in history when the mass of the people profoundly influenced events." It brought the rise of the popular classes and the displacement of the oligarchy that had ruled the country's destiny through almost all of the 19th century. For the first time, the peasants and the working classes were positioned as a real political force with a voice in the country's development. The new state, born in 1920 when the bullets stopped flying and the dust settled, was not democratic in the whole sense of the word, but it was nationalist and popular, not xenophobic; it was revolutionary but with stable institutions. The Mexican Revolution spawned authoritarian leaders, but they were men forged on the battlefield, with a social conscience and willingness to fight for justice and economic equality.

From an economic point of view, the Mexican Revolution was like a second war of independence: it backpedaled the process of big foreign trusts taking over the country's economy. The expression "taking over the country's economy" may seem exaggerated, but looking at Mexico's history through what historians call long-cycle analysis, it is clear that foreign powers, especially the United States, were advancing slowly and inexorably over the country. It was a new form of appropriation, no longer a territorial conquest but economic, through foreign investments and the intensive exploitation of natural resources. In 1910, when Francisco Madero made the call to arms, foreign trusts were controlling Mexican territory and even political decisions, and national workers and companies were increasingly dependent on the US business cycle. Porfirio Díaz tried to slow down that process by approaching Europe, but the Mexican Revolution applied the brakes. The Mexican Revolution influenced other popular movements across the Americas, such as Nicaragua and possibly Cuba.

Diplomatically, the revolution had an achievement as well: always in the shadow of the most powerful country in the world, the United States, the Mexican Revolution freed Mexico from America's hand. In the words of Frank Tannenbaum, one of the first historians of the Mexican Revolution in the 1930s, it brought home "the recognition that Mexicans were masters in their own house," putting an end to the fear, which had always been present, of being absorbed by the first world power on the planet.

Most of the great original revolutionaries did not live to see the result of their struggle, but its younger followers, those who rode with Madero, Villa, and Zapata—people like Lázaro Cárdenas, Salvador Alvarado, and José Vasconcelos—created the new Mexican nation.

After a hundred years of calamities, the country found a route that could accommodate everyone.

Epilogue – The Head of Pancho Villa and the Hand of Obregón

And what happened to Pancho Villa? In 1920, when his enemy Carranza died, Villa was a shadow of the great general who once had swept Mexico. For four years, he traveled the roads and passages between the mountains of northern Mexico with a few hundred men, robbing and breaking into estates and villages to survive. The Americans wanted him and put a price on his head; the Carrancistas wanted him too, and the new leaders of Mexico—Álvaro Obregón and his men from Sonora—distrusted him. Villa could be an outlaw, but he was the last great heavyweight of the revolution still alive, and he had demonstrated his ability to summon people around him. The provisional president, Adolfo de la Huerta, raised the reward for Pancho Villa, dead or alive.

In 1920, Villa decided to negotiate. A meeting was arranged, but when the government envoy tried to kill him, Villa proclaimed that things had not changed and that he was going to continue the fight. However, he was certain that the new generation did not know what to do with him, whether to kill him or render honors to him. He crossed the desert, seized more weapons and provisions where nobody expected to see him, and, from a position of strength, he made a new proposal to President Adolfo de la Huerta. The president, eager to pacify the north, offered him the hacienda of Canutillo and a personal escort of fifty men paid by the government, although he demanded that Pancho withdraw completely from political activities. Although reluctant at first, Álvaro Obregón, who in a few months would be the new president of Mexico, accepted the pact and made peace with Villa. The US government welcomed the deal because that meant that peace would finally come to Mexico. To the relief of the Mexican government, the United States did not request the extradition of Pancho Villa. The only one to protest bitterly was Britain's secretary of war, Winston Churchill, who called him a murderer and launched threats against Mexico if justice was not sought for the death of a British citizen in 1914.

Villa marched triumphantly with his last men from Coahuila to Durango to enter his safe haven, where he would spend his last years as a simple farmer. Many people went out to see him and cheer him on his march. That man had swept all of northern Mexico in response to Madero's call; he had barely escaped from being shot by Victoriano Huerta, had fled from a prison in Mexico City, had formed the largest army in the history of his country. He had sat in the presidential chair and had despised it, had become America's dearest only to later fall from its grace, and had invaded the United States and became a desperado persecuted by the US Army. But deep in his heart, he had the dream that once the dictators fell and justice was done for the people, he could withdraw and "grow corn and raise cattle until I die among my companions who have suffered so much with me" according to his words to journalist John Reed. "They used to call me a bandit, and I suppose some still call me that," he said to another journalist, Edmond Behr. "My heart is clean. My sole ambition was to disburden Mexico from the [social] class that has oppressed it, and to give the people a chance to know what real liberty means."

The last 800 Villistas surrendered their weapons to the federal government, and Villa occupied a 64,000-hectare hacienda in the state of Durango, a well-watered and fertile area, far away enough to provide him with some protection. Throughout his entire career, he had made enough enemies to know that his safety was one of the most delicate elements to consider. At the hacienda, Villa and his men rebuilt the decayed buildings, stables, and cellars. They put in telephone lines, a mill, and a school for 300 students for the dozens of children Villa had with different wives, plus his soldiers' children and those of the neighboring towns. He baptized the school with the name of Felipe Ángeles, his late faithful general. "If I were in charge of things," he told journalist Frazier Hunt, "I would build a lot of schools in cities and towns, and I would also put a school in every ranch." Sometimes Villa would be present in the classroom and asked teachers to read biographies of famous men to him. Another journalist who visited the hacienda saw that Dante's Divine *Comedy* and a geography text were among his bedside books.

Villa imposed strict conditions on everyone who lived in the Canutillo hacienda. The bell rang at four o'clock in the morning, and everybody had to work the land. Villa supervised the work and sometimes took the yoke himself. He severely punished any robbery with execution. He told his men that he wanted to be able to leave a bag of gold in one place and find it in the same place when he returned, and he warned them that if he had taught them to kill and steal, he wanted them to rehabilitate. *The New York Times* recorded, "Pancho Villa, the former bandit, is a peace-loving, hard-working contented rancher, without political ambitions and imbued with a sincere desire to help his people." True to his word, he stayed away from politics, and if any conspirators visited him to talk him into starting another revolution, he turned them over to Álvaro Obregón. The one-armed man of Celaya was pleased with these signs of obedience from the only general who could cast a shadow on him. Unlike his boss Carranza, Obregón was a practical man with a political nose, a sense of opportunity, and an unchallenged personal charisma. When he came to the presidency in 1920—with a more prominent belly, receding hairline, and a pointed mustache that was beginning to turn white—he was no longer the handsome general of the Mexican Revolution who had won his battles with his army of indomitable Yaqui. But he kept his ability to navigate difficult waters.

In 1922, when more generals were preparing for the presidential elections, Villa, a living legend, made the mistake of talking about politics with a journalist. Even worse, he launched a veiled threat. "I am a real soldier," he said. "I can mobilize 40,000 soldiers in 40 minutes. There are thousands of Mexicans who are still my followers." And then he gave his support to candidate Adolfo de la Huerta, the man who had pardoned him, and not to Plutarco Elías Calles, the president's appointed candidate. On July 20th, 1923, Villa got into his car with a reduced escort of four and headed for the city of Parral, eighty kilometers (almost fifty miles) away. Villa and his guards noticed that the streets of Parral were unusually deserted. At some point, an old man passed in front of the car, shouting, "Viva Villa!" and then shots were heard from all directions, piercing the vehicle. Villa was shot four times, but just to be sure, one of his assassins went to the shattered Ford and put a bullet into his head. A horrified girl of thirteen saw the scene, and she ran through the streets of Parral, crying, "They just shot Pancho Villa!" The man who was believed to have been invincible lay with his body pierced in a horrific position, half of it coming out of the car's window. The corpse was exhibited at the Hotel Hidalgo in Parral. Someone had taken off his shirt, and the expression on his face is of deep exhaustion.

Villa was buried in Parral, but even after his death, he demonstrated that he could be, as Pershing would say, everywhere and nowhere. In 1926, they found the grave had been violated, the coffin destroyed. The body was there, but the head had been removed. It was never recovered. Who was interested in the head of Pancho Villa? Theories range from the American government, Yale University, an auction house, and one of Villa's multiple enemies. Villa's reputation remained as a bandit in official history until the 1970s, after enough time had passed, when the rest of the body was exhumed and taken to a place of honor in Mexico City: the emblematic Monument to the Revolution. Or so they thought. In

1931, one of his widows, fearing that grave robbers would continue to desecrate his tomb and body, placed Villa's remains in an unmarked grave and replaced them with an anonymous woman who had died of cancer at the Parral hospital. When they opened the tomb in 1976, they found jewelry and fragments of a woman's dress.

The hand that Álvaro Obregón had lost in his final confrontation with Villa in central Mexico also had a macabre adventure. When his doctor Enrique Osornio amputated the arm on the battlefield, among the flying bullets, he kept the general's hand in a jar with formalin. The hand reached the state of Sinaloa, and not knowing what to do with it, the doctor gave it to a military friend of Obregón's, who told him that he was not very interested in hanging onto it. In a strange twist of fate, the jar was stolen by a prostitute, and the severed hand ended up in a brothel in downtown Mexico City, where it was found years later by the same doctor who amputated the arm. He took it and gave it to a former collaborator of Obregón, who convinced President Lázaro Cárdenas (1934–1940) to build a monument for the hand in the restaurant where Obregón was assassinated in 1928. The restaurant was demolished, and the place became a macabre mausoleum that displayed the leader's right hand, which, by then, was already yellow, crimped, misshapen, and inflated like a balloon. It stayed there for many years until his descendants, surely horrified by that unspeakable monument, requested the hand and cremated it in 1989.

The "villain" of this story, Victoriano Huerta, rests in a modest grave in the Evergreen Cemetery in El Paso, Texas, less than one mile away from the border, still unable to reach his country. At night, the tomb is visited by members of El Paso paranormal associations because they attribute powers to it and believe that, from the grave, Huerta continues to emanate "evil forces."

In some way, the strange story of Pancho Villa's head, Obregón's hand, and Huerta's grave are all metaphors for the Mexican Revolution: its heroes and villains, dead and buried, their exploits and felonies, now extinguished, continue to inspire respect, fear, curiosity, and devotion. Just like the Mexican Revolution. The revolutionaries' bones might be in a monument, or they might be lost, perhaps appropriated by the state, institutionalized, or forgotten under a humble tombstone, but the men's ideals and lessons, one hundred years after the end of the storm, remain intact.

Here's another book by Captivating History
that you might be interested in

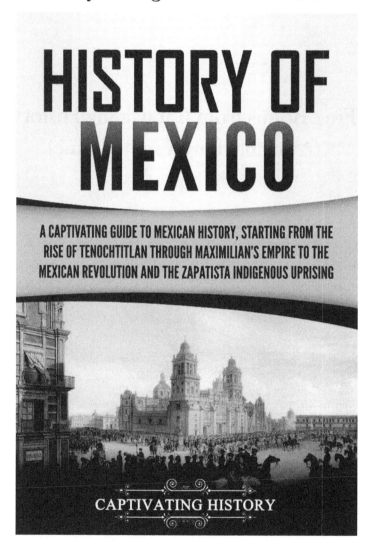

HISTORY OF MEXICO

A CAPTIVATING GUIDE TO MEXICAN HISTORY, STARTING FROM THE
RISE OF TENOCHTITLAN THROUGH MAXIMILIAN'S EMPIRE TO THE
MEXICAN REVOLUTION AND THE ZAPATISTA INDIGENOUS UPRISING

CAPTIVATING HISTORY

Free Bonus from Captivating History (Available for a Limited time)

Hi History Lovers!

Now you have a chance to join our exclusive history list so you can get your first history ebook for free as well as discounts and a potential to get more history books for free! Simply visit the link below to join.

Captivatinghistory.com/ebook

Also, make sure to follow us on Facebook, Twitter and Youtube by searching for Captivating History.

Bibliography

Blaisdell, L. "Henry Lane Wilson and the Overthrow of Madero." *The Southwestern Social Science Quarterly*, 1962.

Brenner, Anita. *The Wind that Swept Mexico*. University of Texas Press, 1971.

Gilly, Adolfo. *The Mexican Revolution*. The New Press, 2005.

Katz, Friedrich. *The Life and Times of Pancho Villa*. Stanford University Press, 1998.

Katz, Friedrich. *The Secret War in Mexico*. University of Chicago, 1984.

Knight, Alan. *The Mexican Revolution*, Vol 1-3. University of Nebraska Press, 1990.

Meyer, M. "The Mexican-German Conspiracy of 1915." *The Americas*, 23(1), 76-89, 1966.

Meyer, M. *Huerta*. University of Nebraska Press, 1972.

Mraz, John. *Photographing the Mexican Revolution. Commitments, Testimonies, Icons*. University of Texas Press, 2012.

Reed, John. *Insurgent Mexico*. Red and Black Publishers, 2009.

Welsome, Eileen. *The General and the Jaguar: Pershing's Hunt for Pancho Villa: A True Story of Revolution and Revenge*. Little, Brown and Company, 2009.

Womack, John. *Zapata and the Mexican Revolution*. Vintage, 2011.

Guzmán, Martín Luis. *The Eagle and the Serpent.*
Knight, Alan. (1990) *The Mexican Revolution.* Vol 1-3. University of Nebraska Press.
Tuchman, Barbara. (1985) *The Zimmermann Telegram.* Random House.

Made in the USA
Las Vegas, NV
30 June 2024

91686991R00069